This Book
BELONGS TO

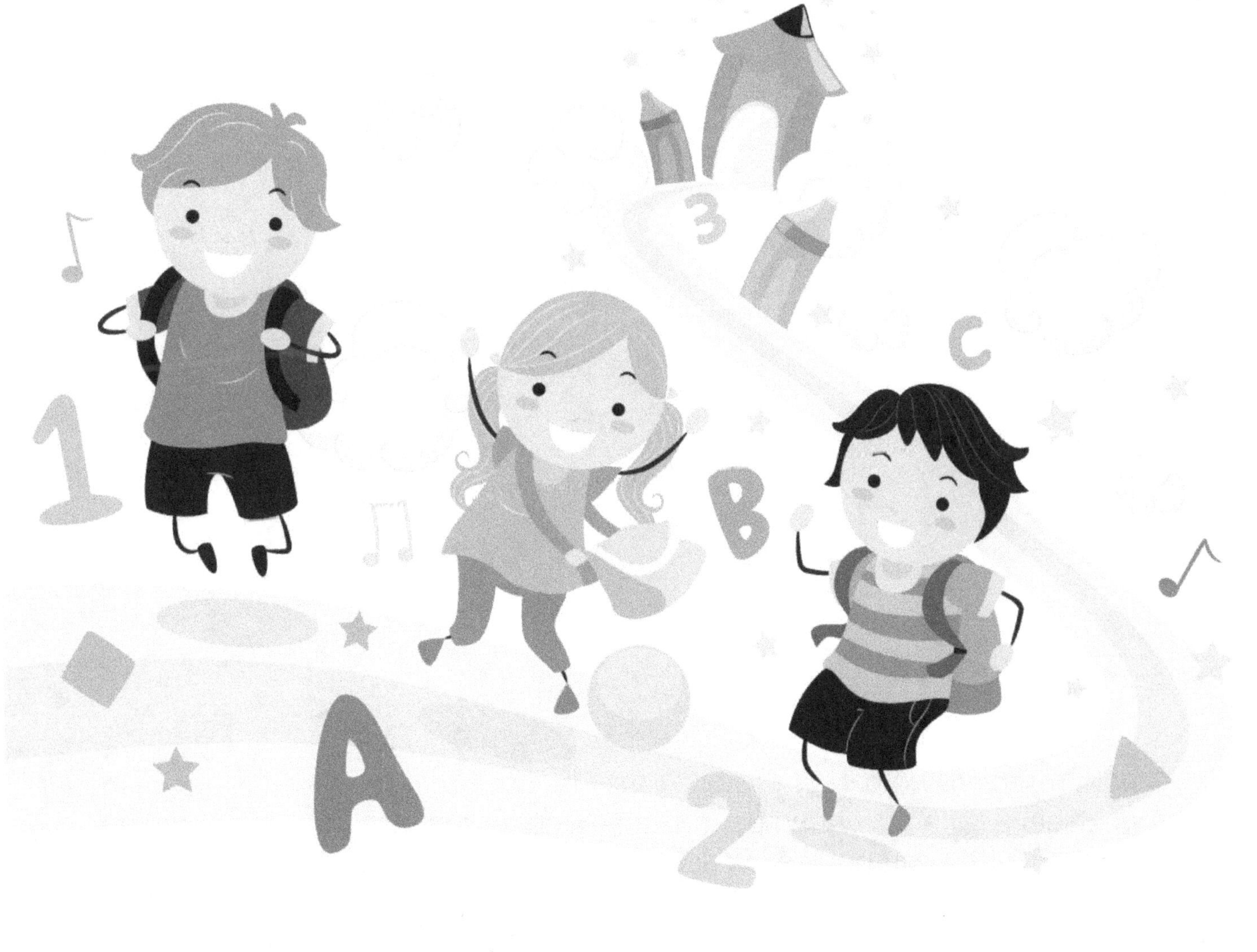

____

____

____

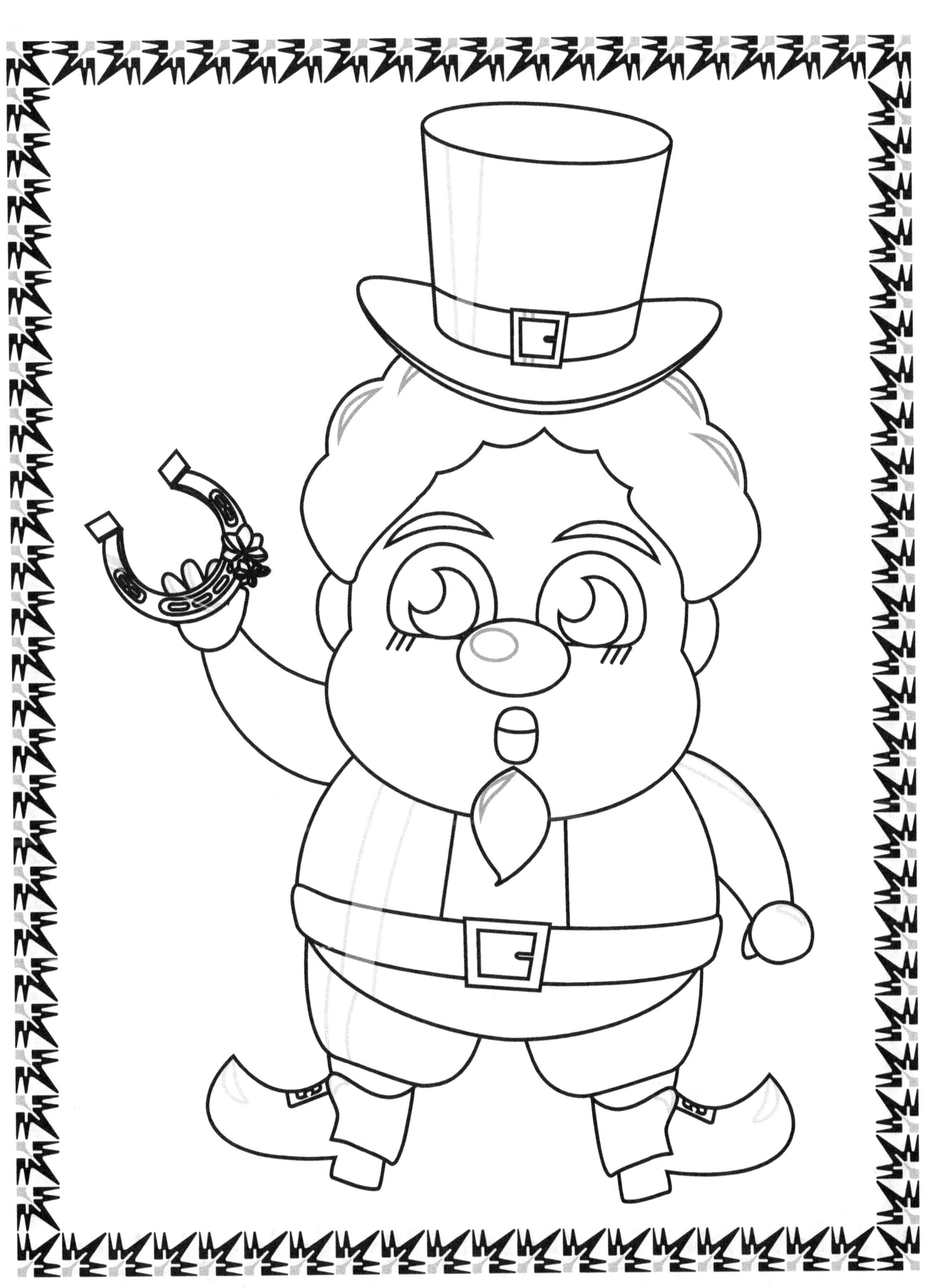

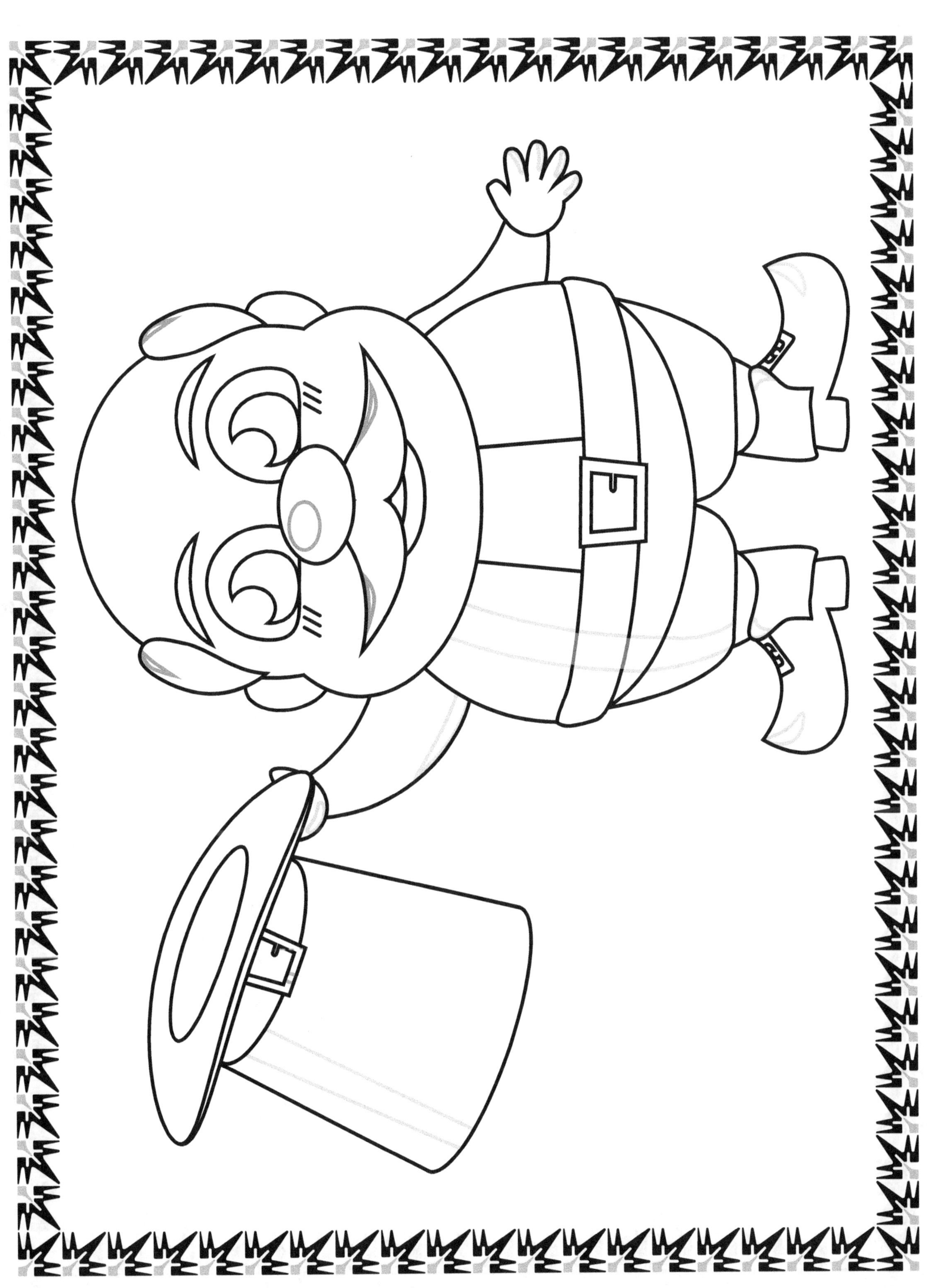

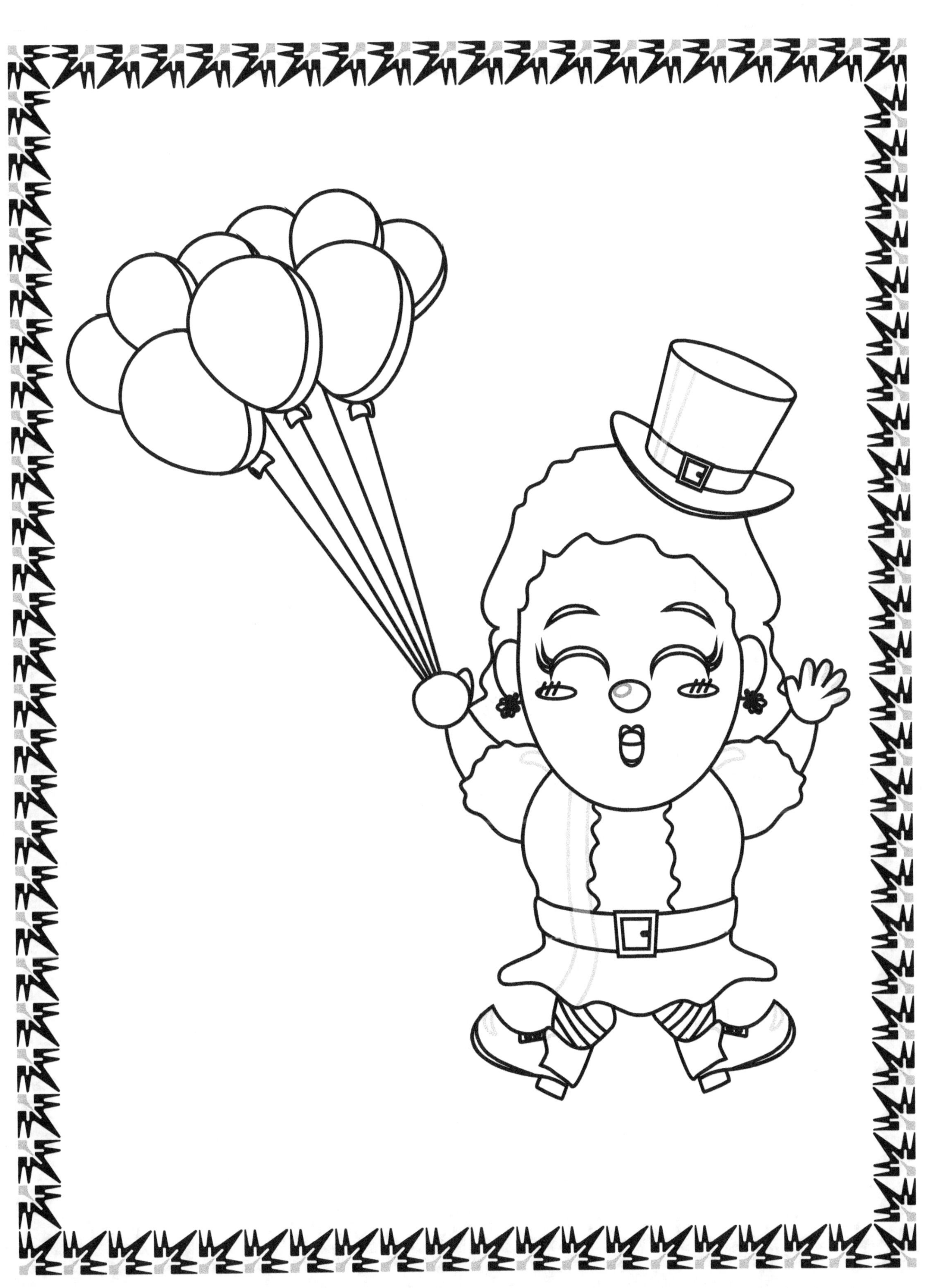

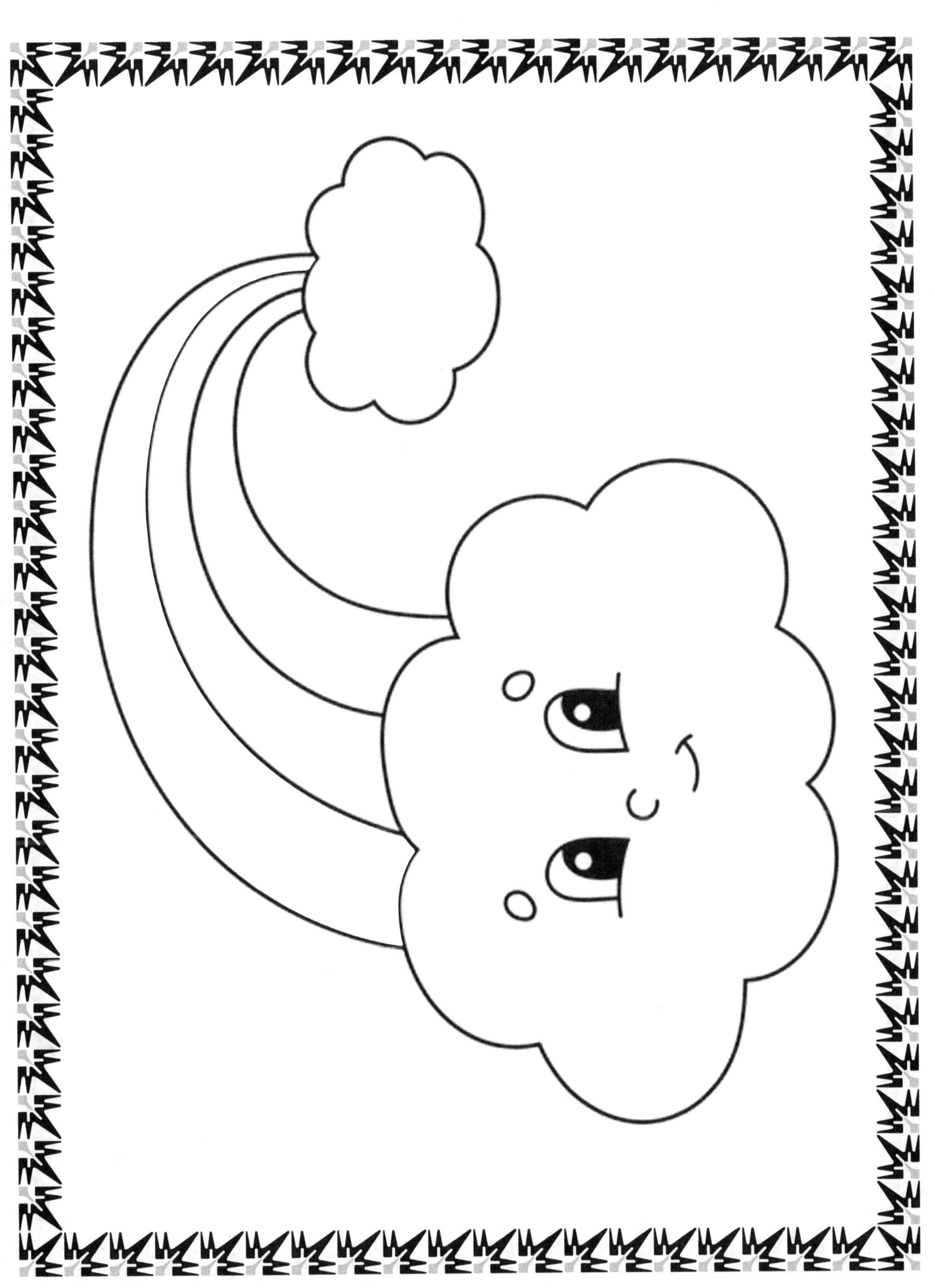

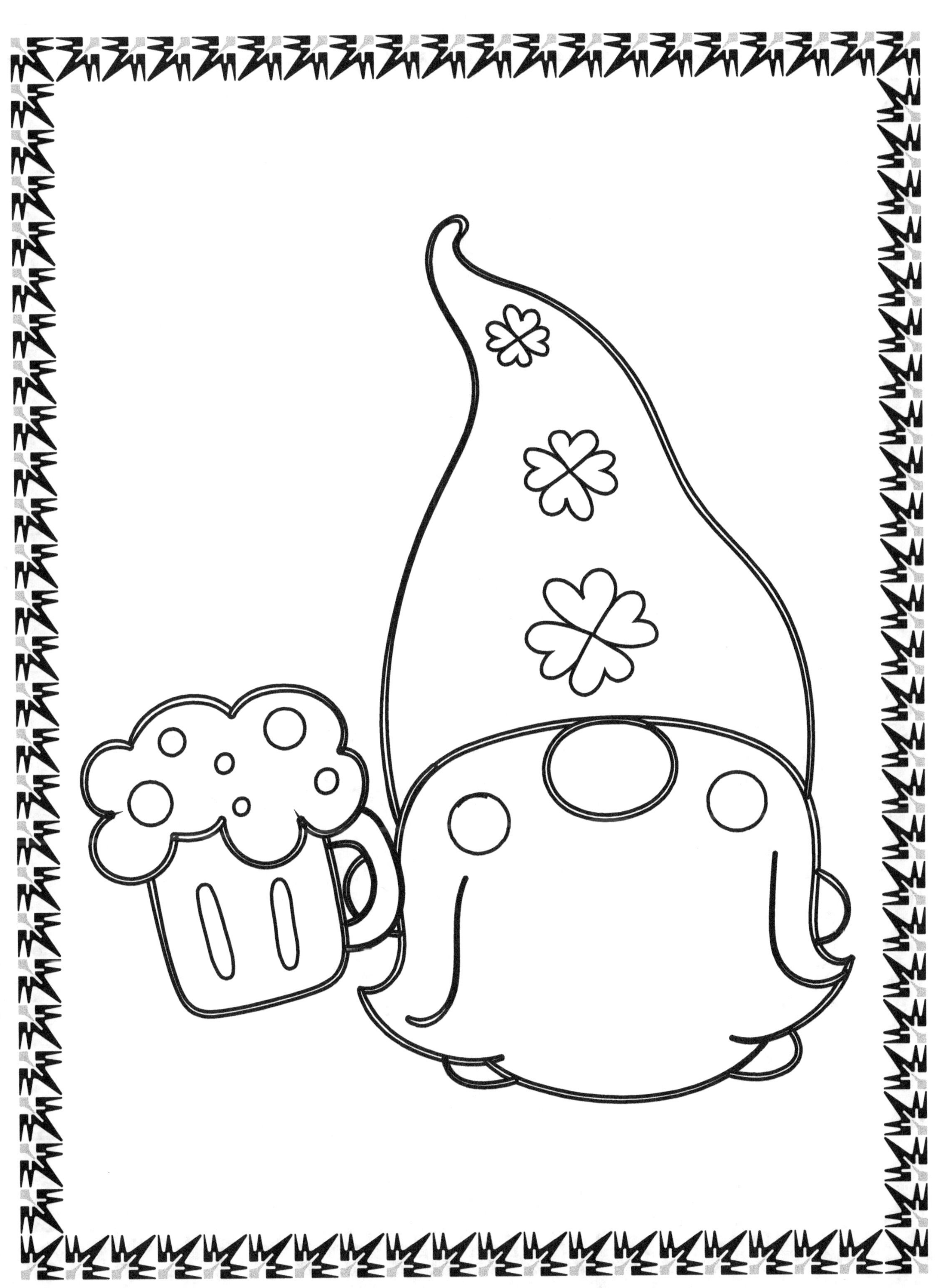

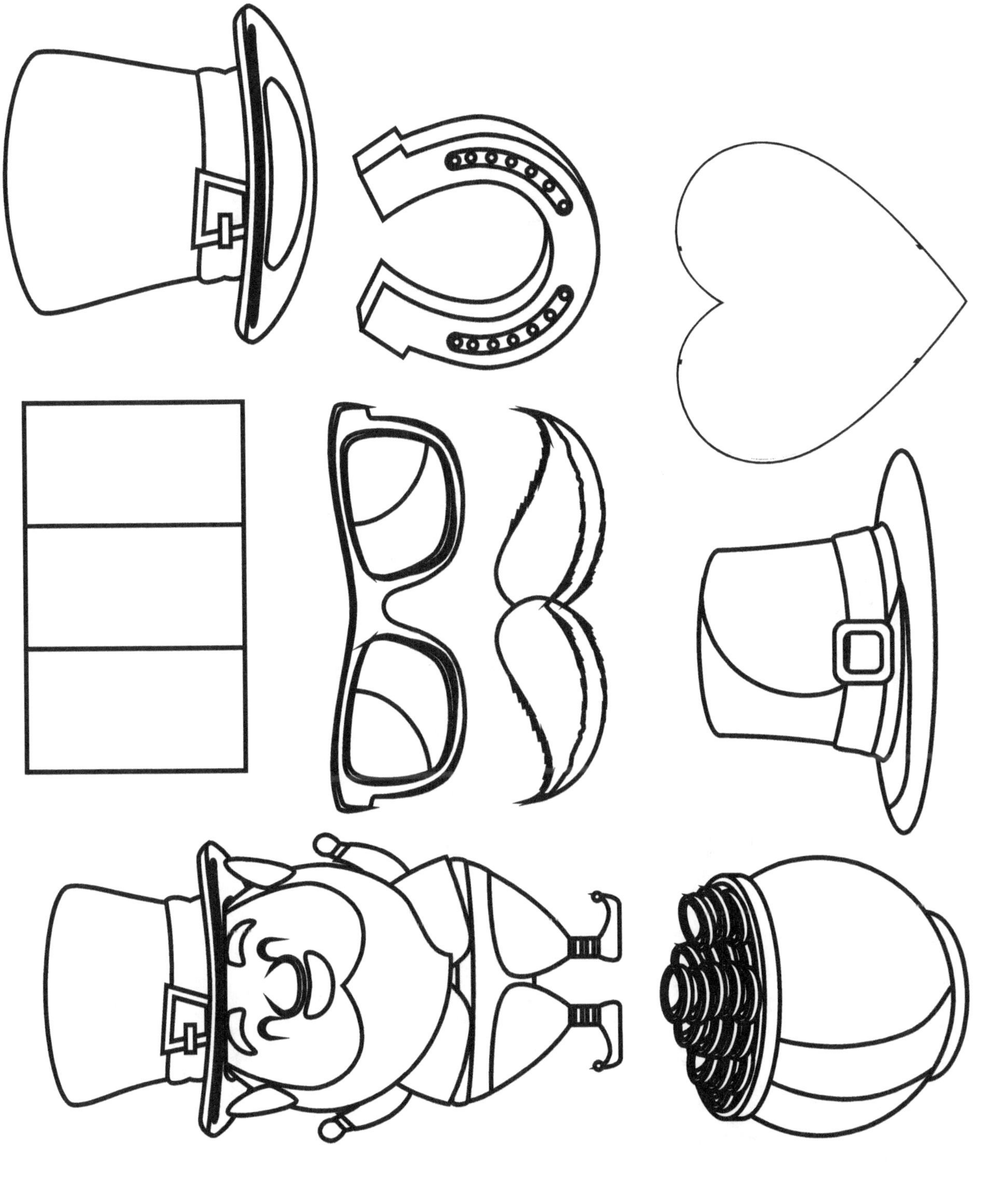

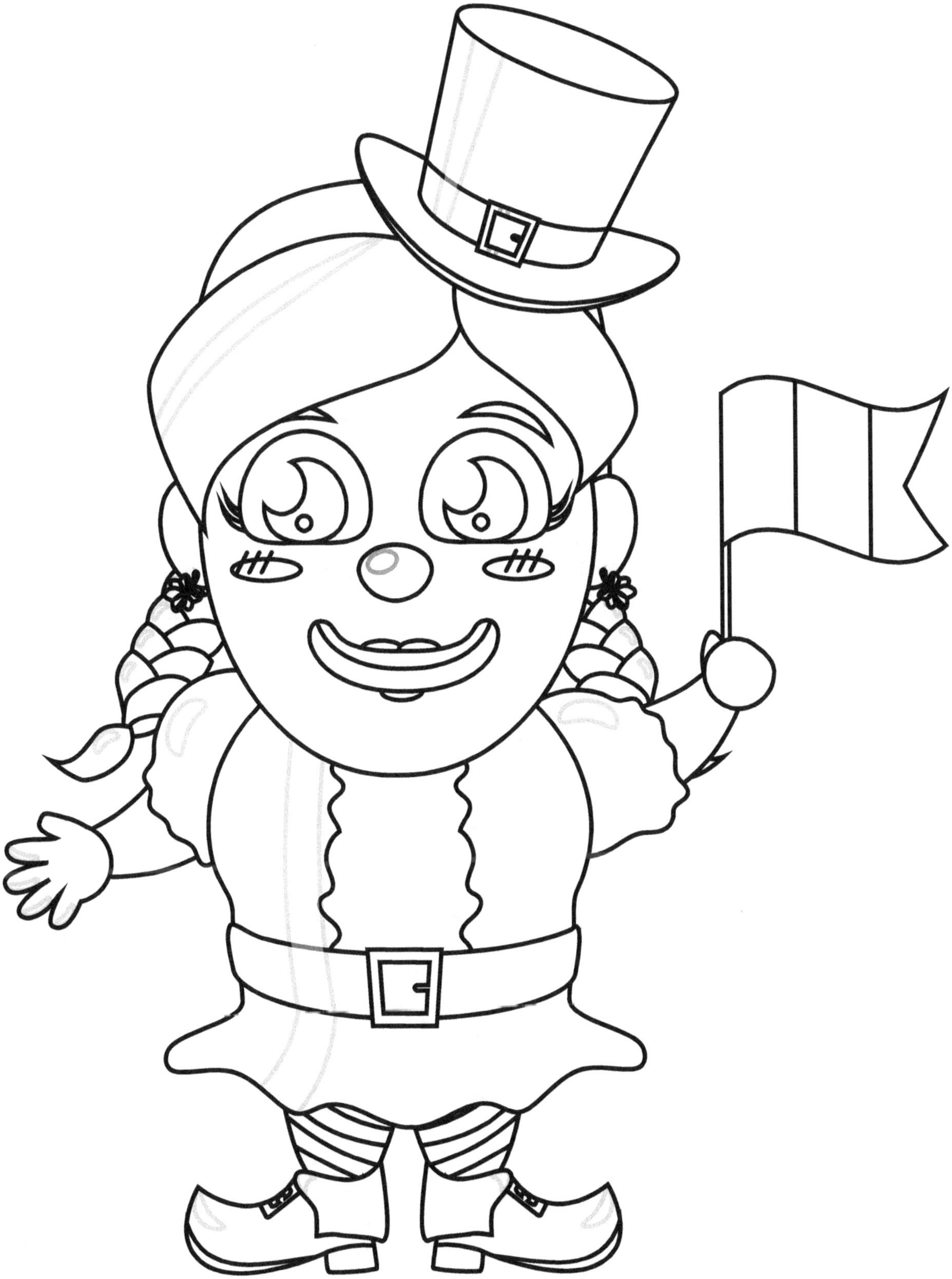

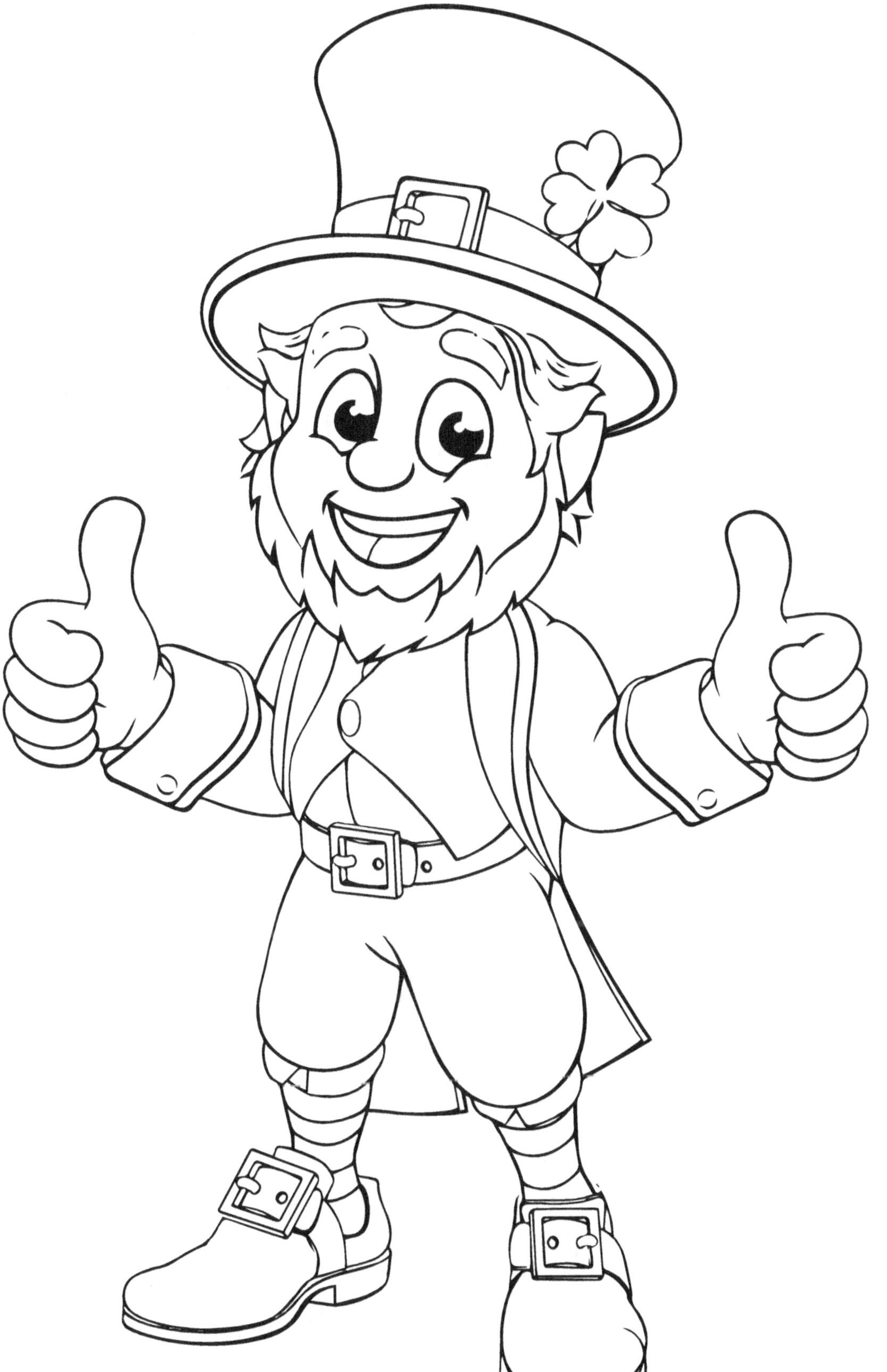

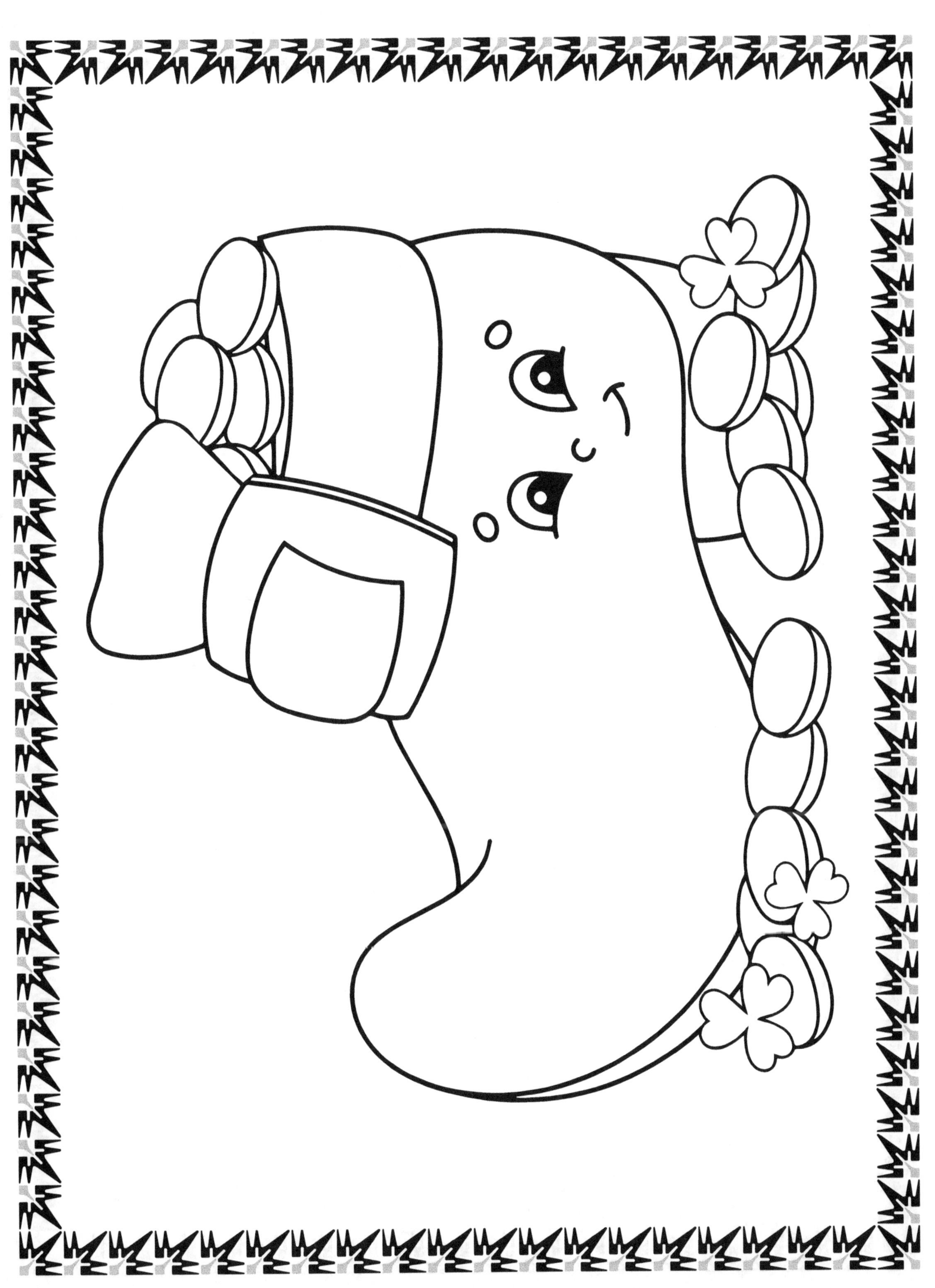

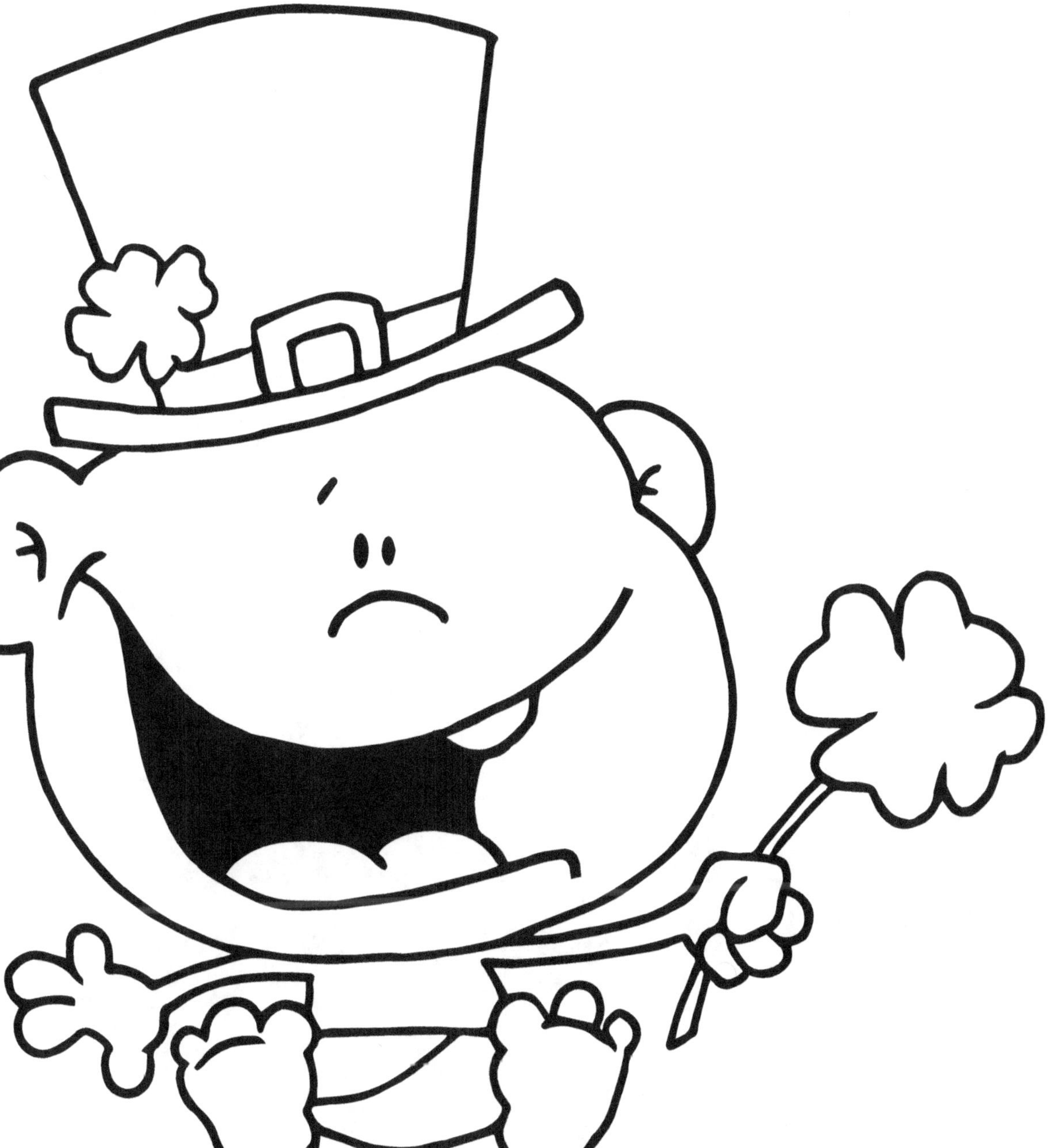

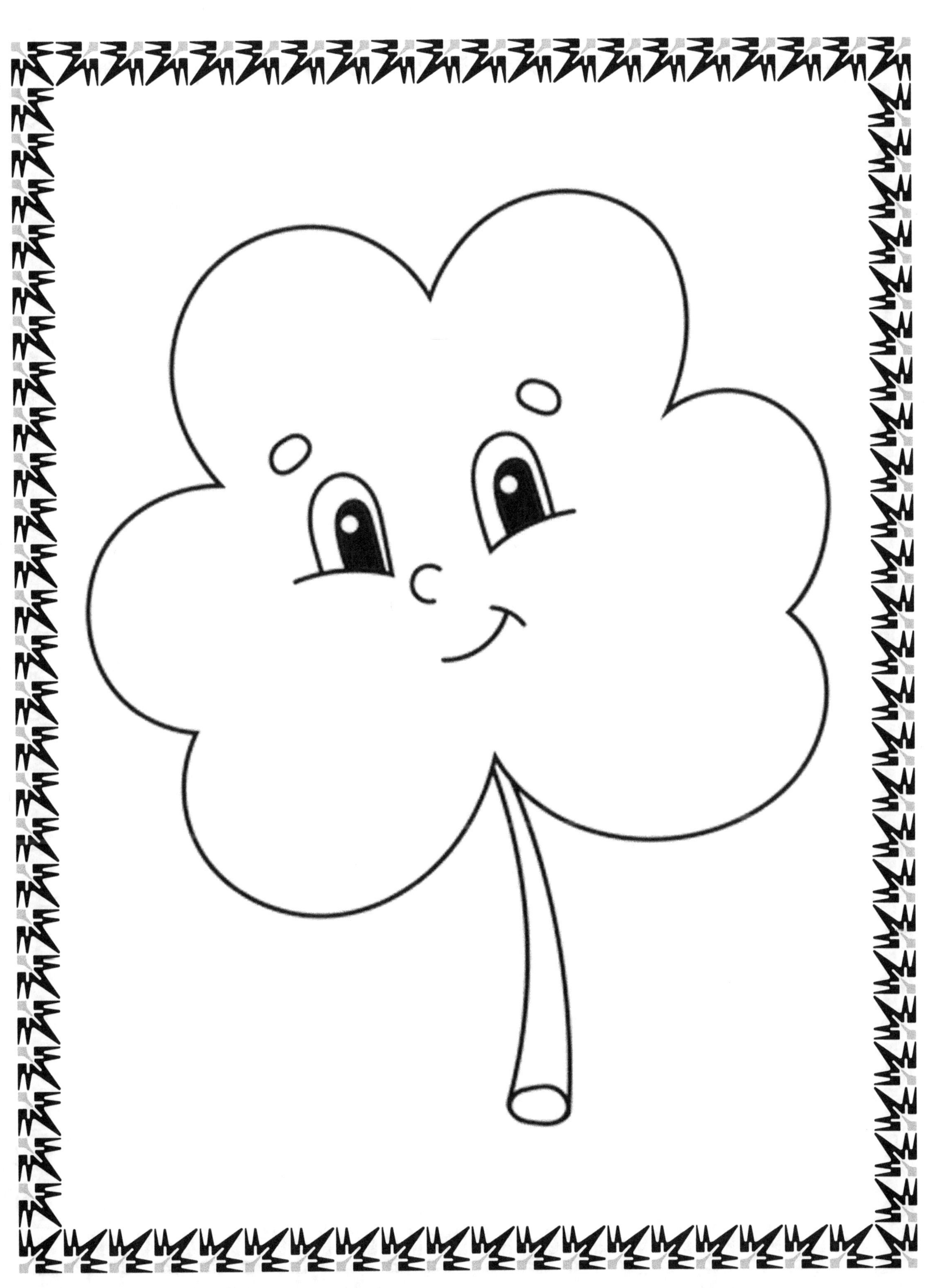

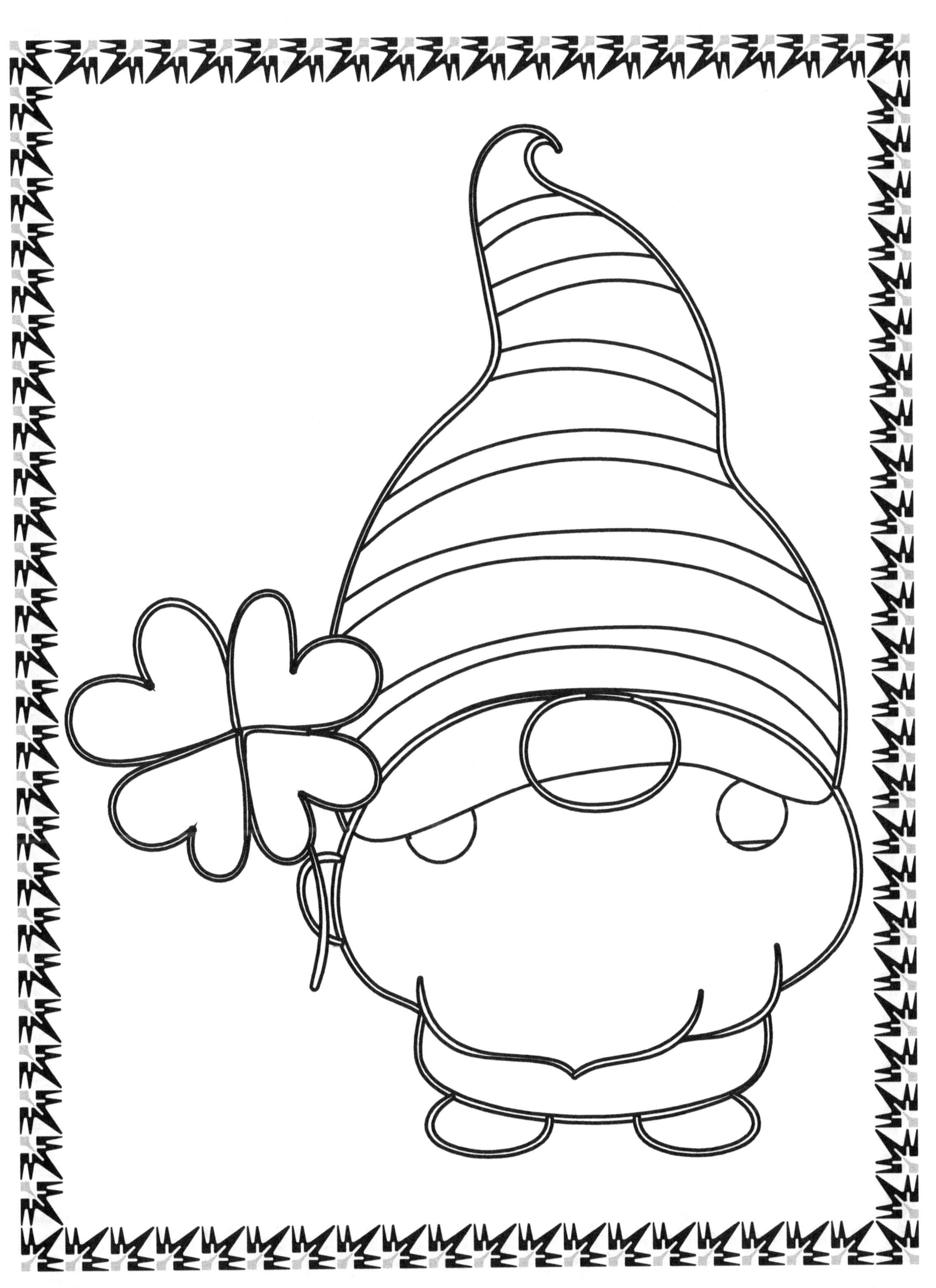

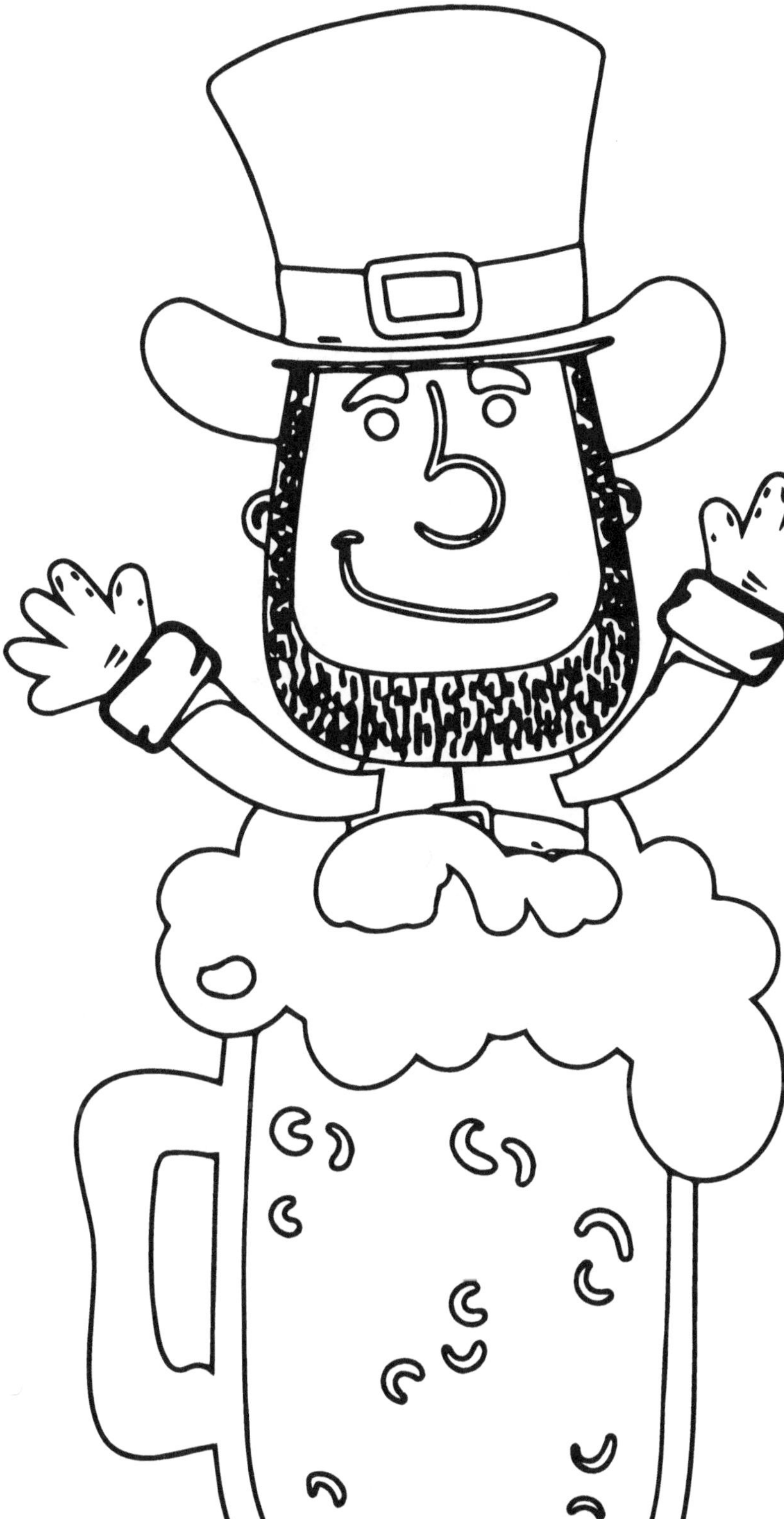

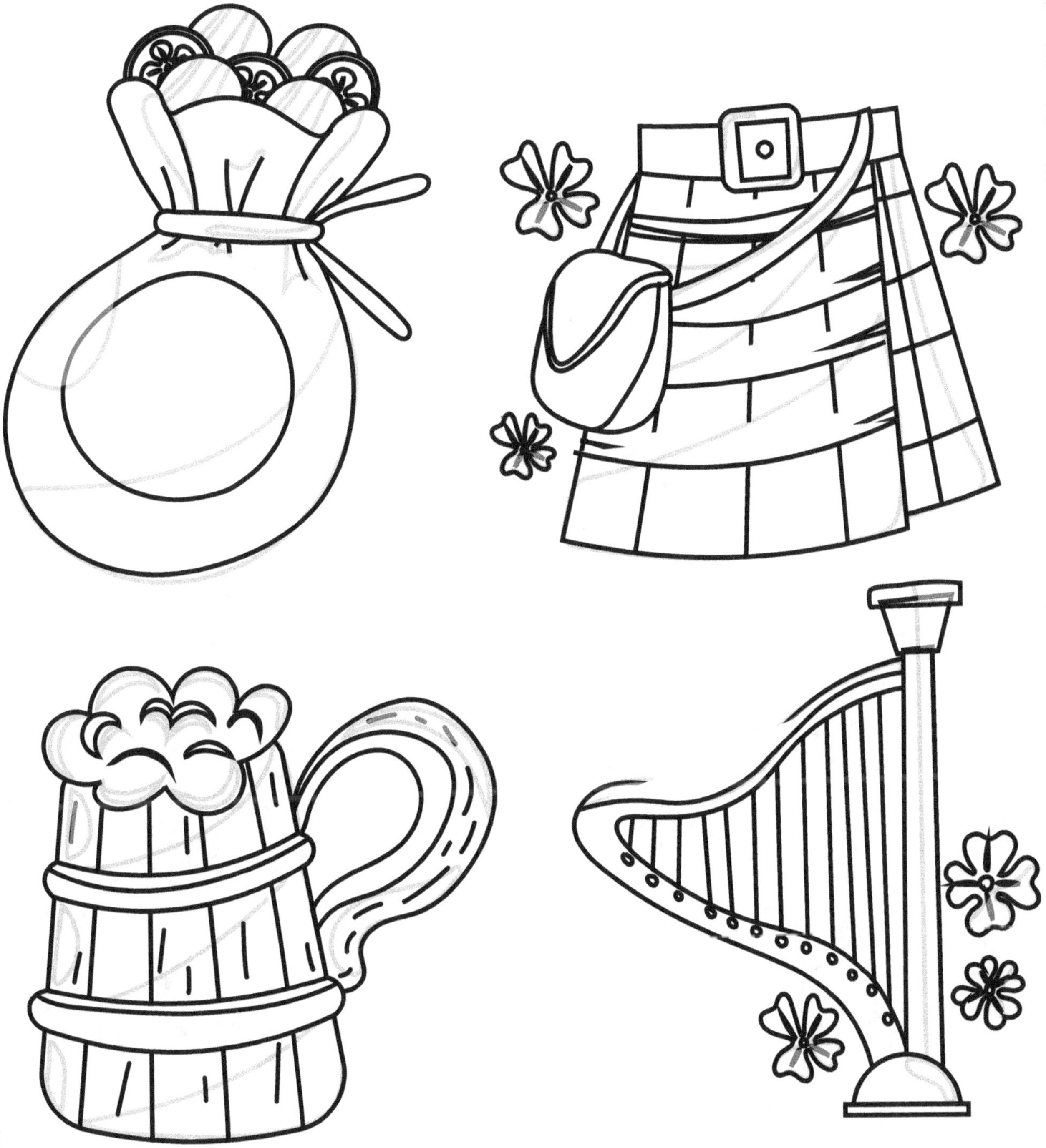

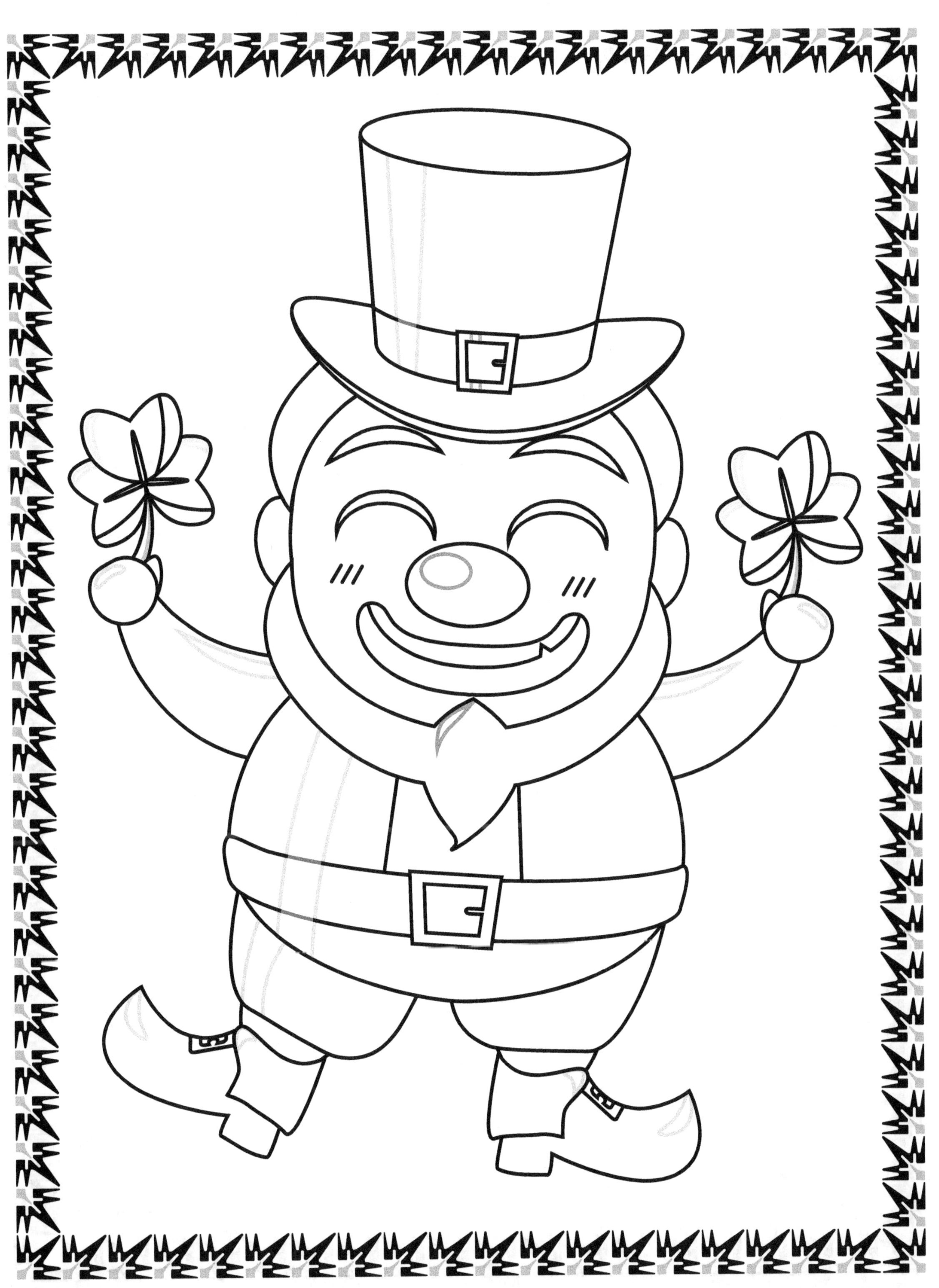

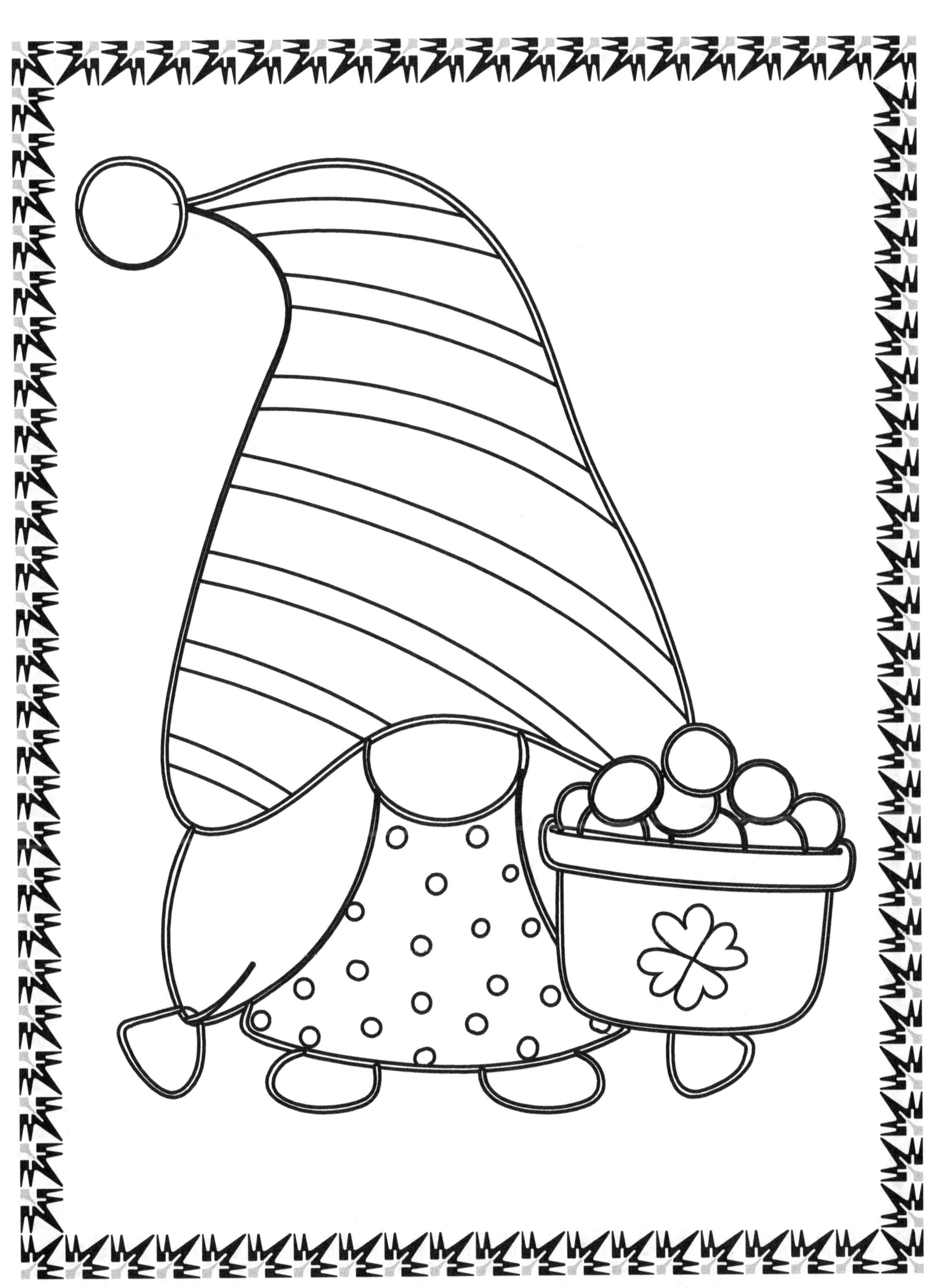

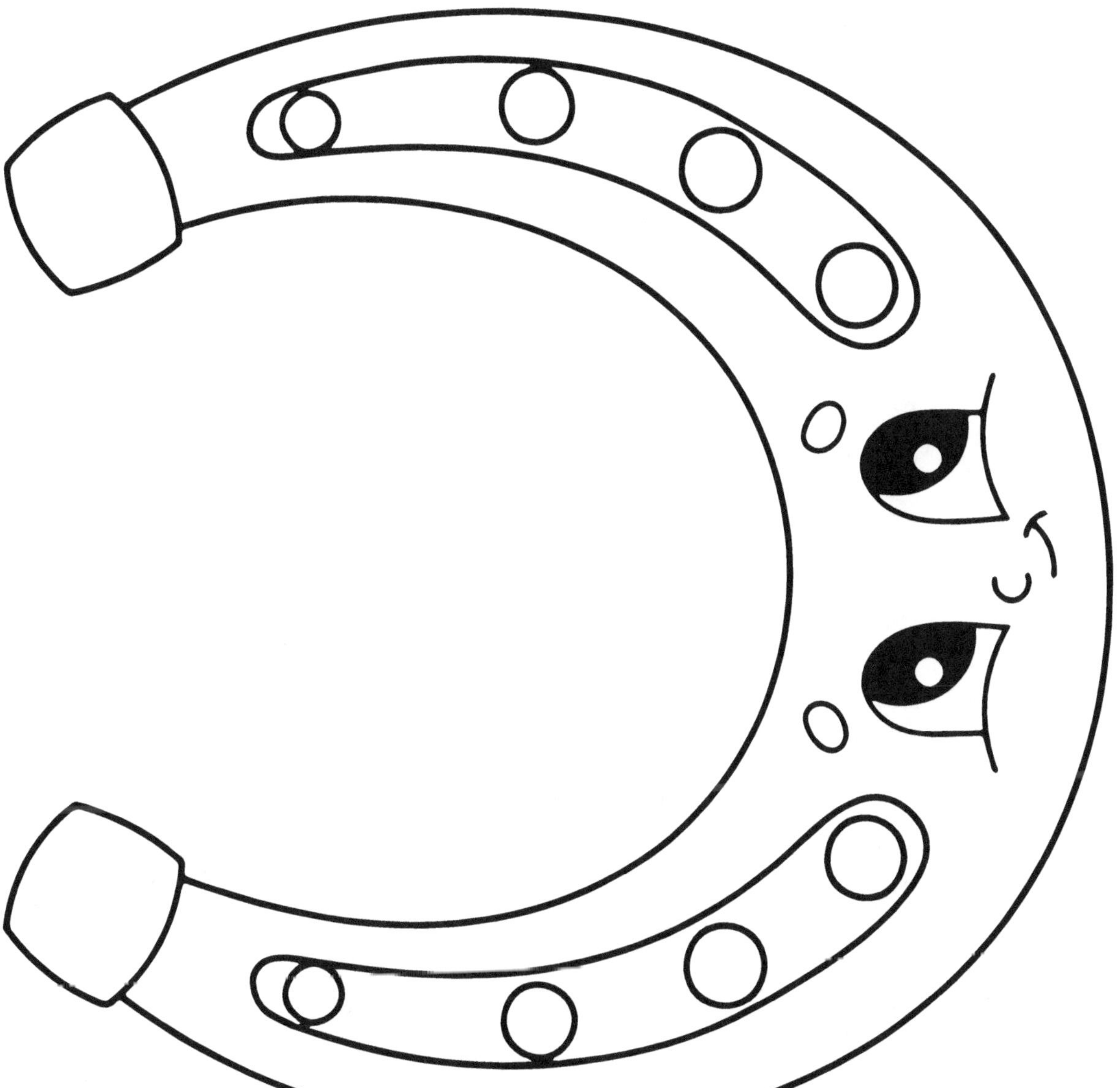

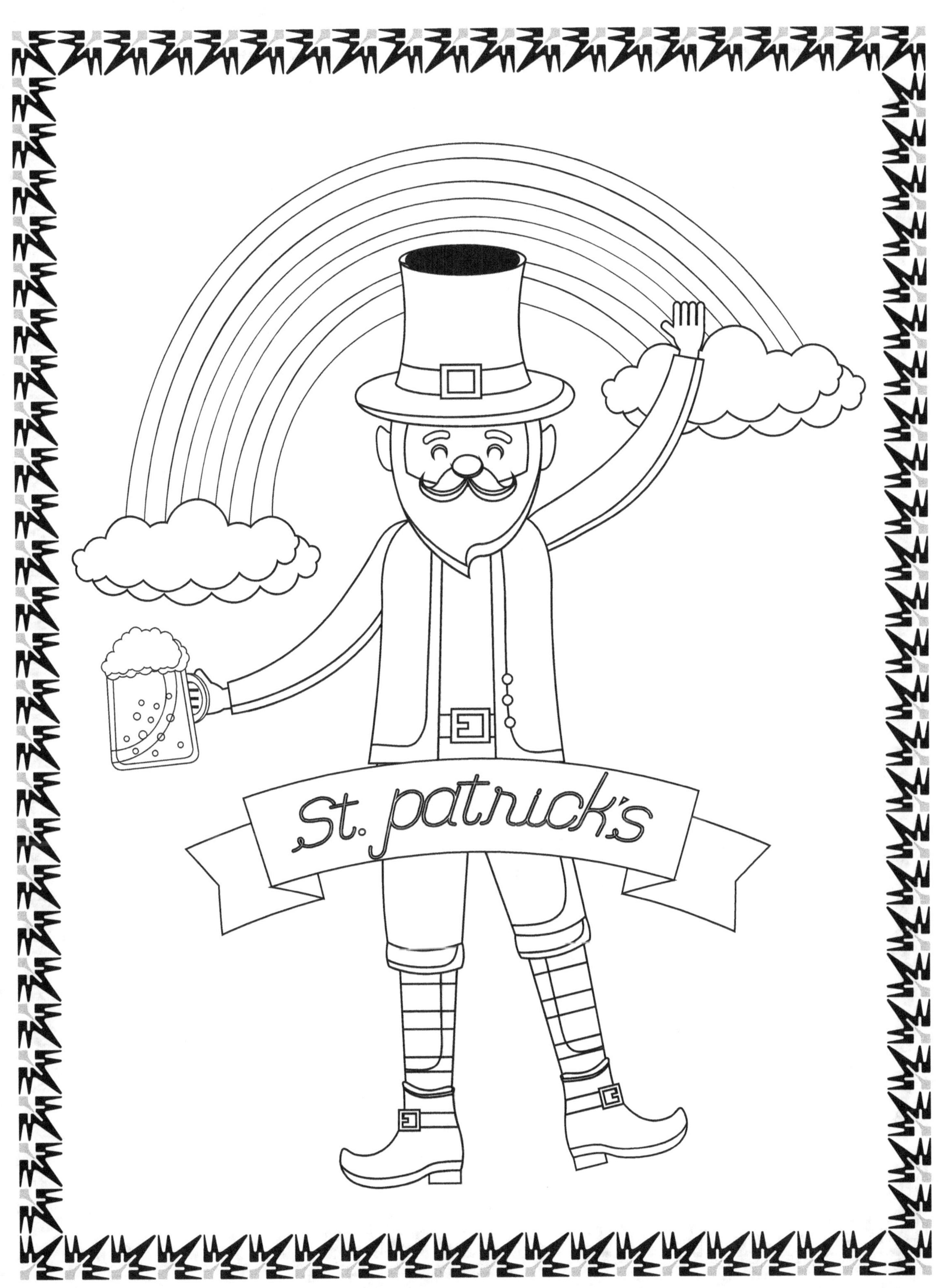

St. patrick's

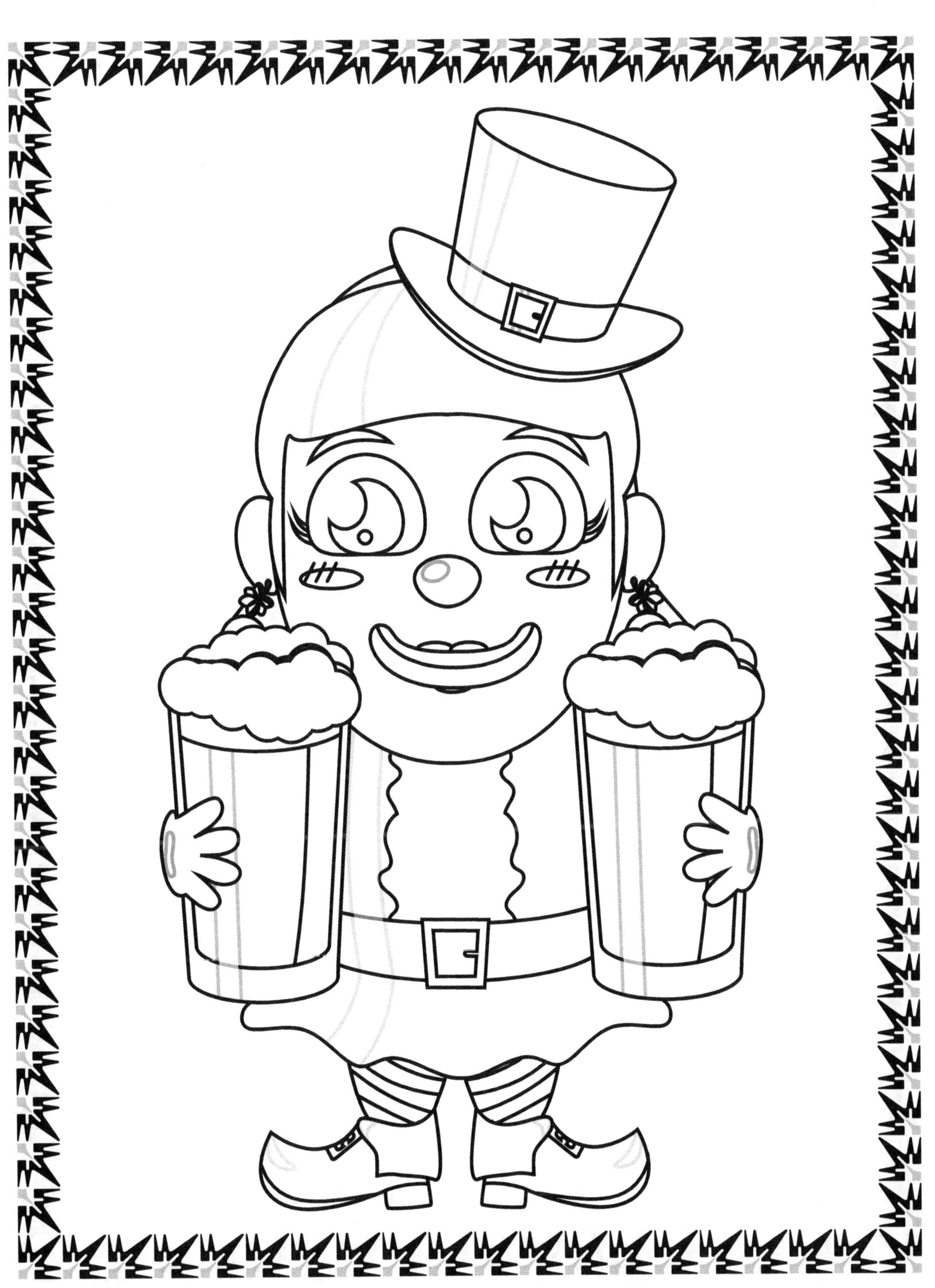

St. Patrick'sDay

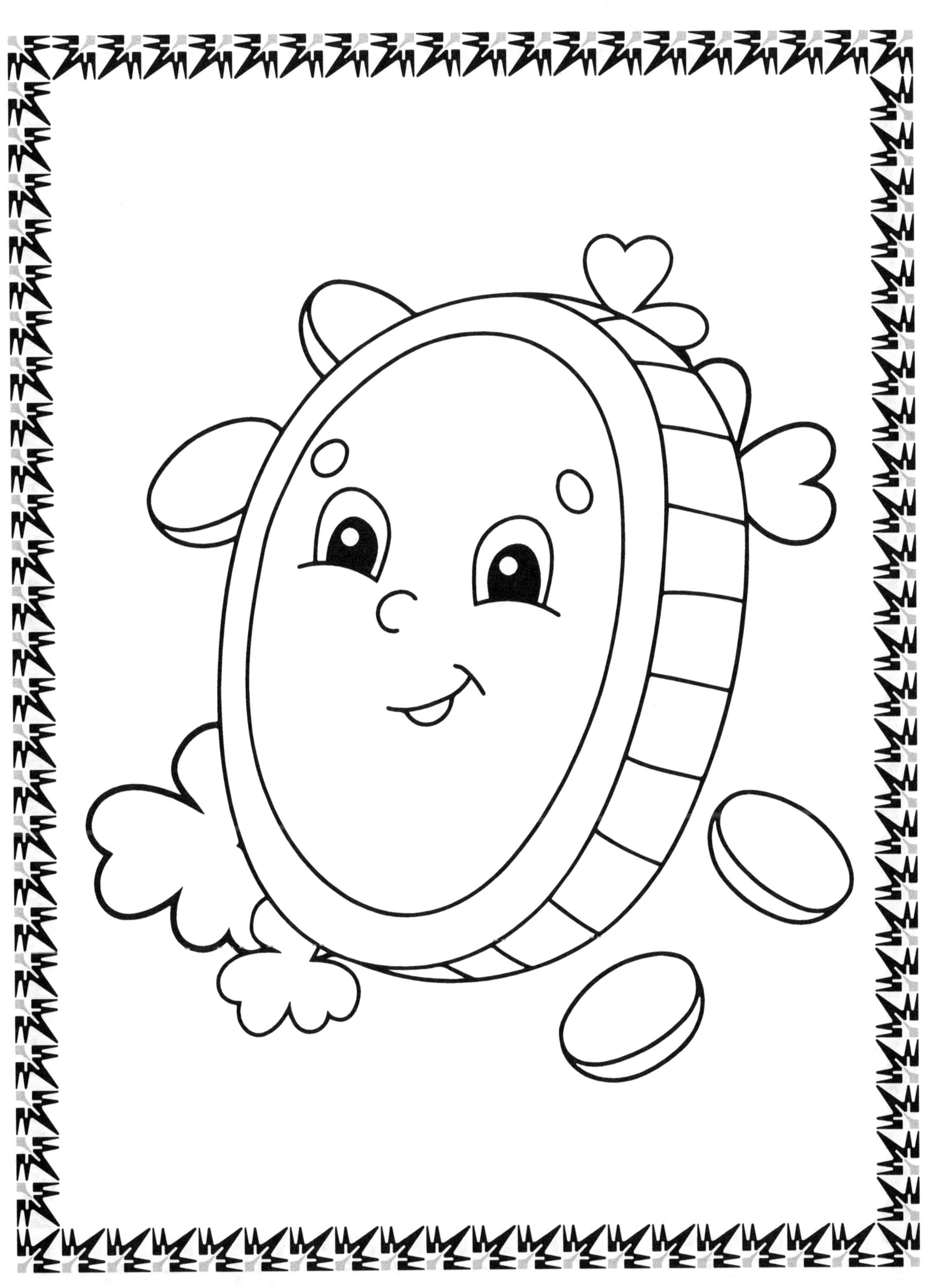

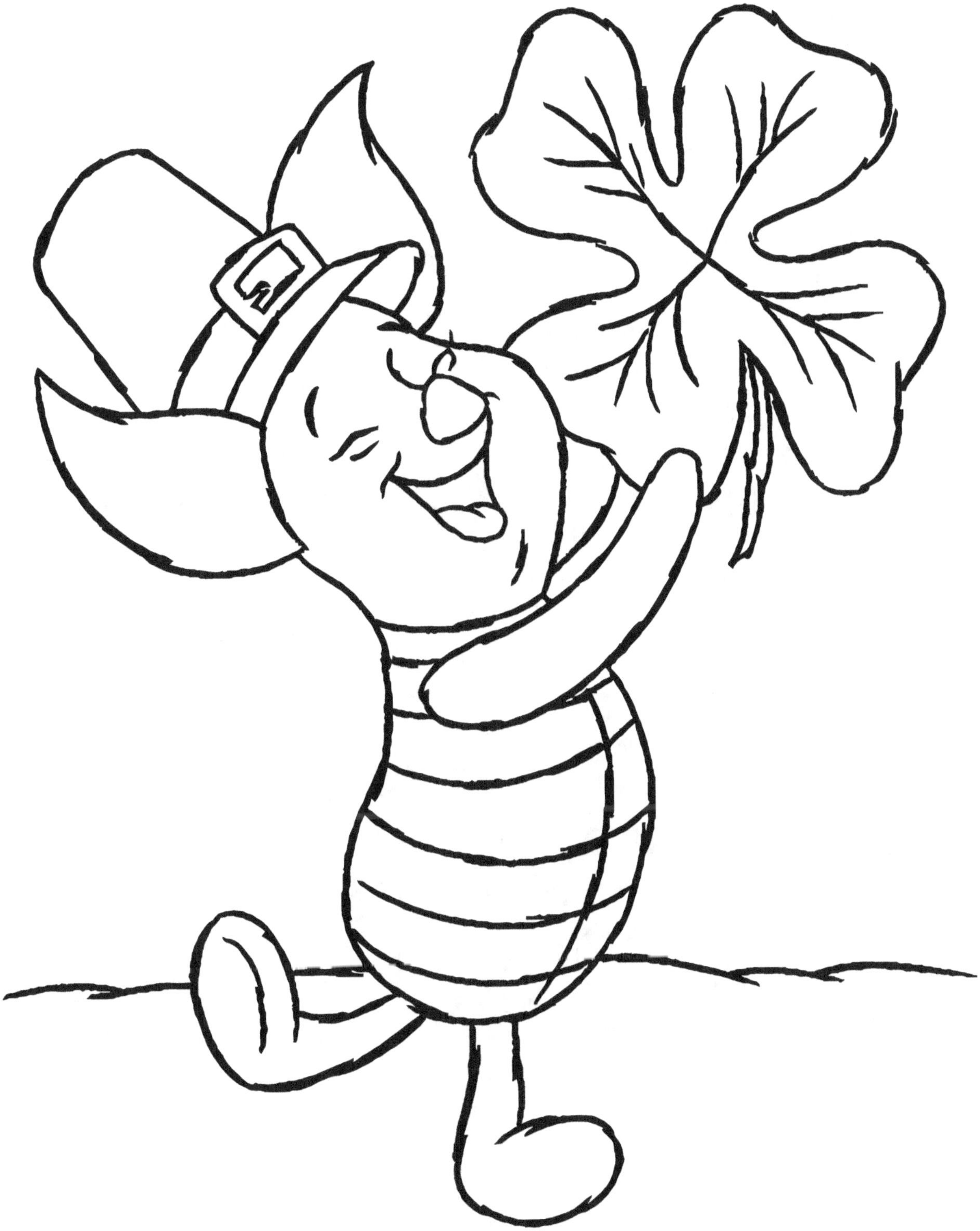

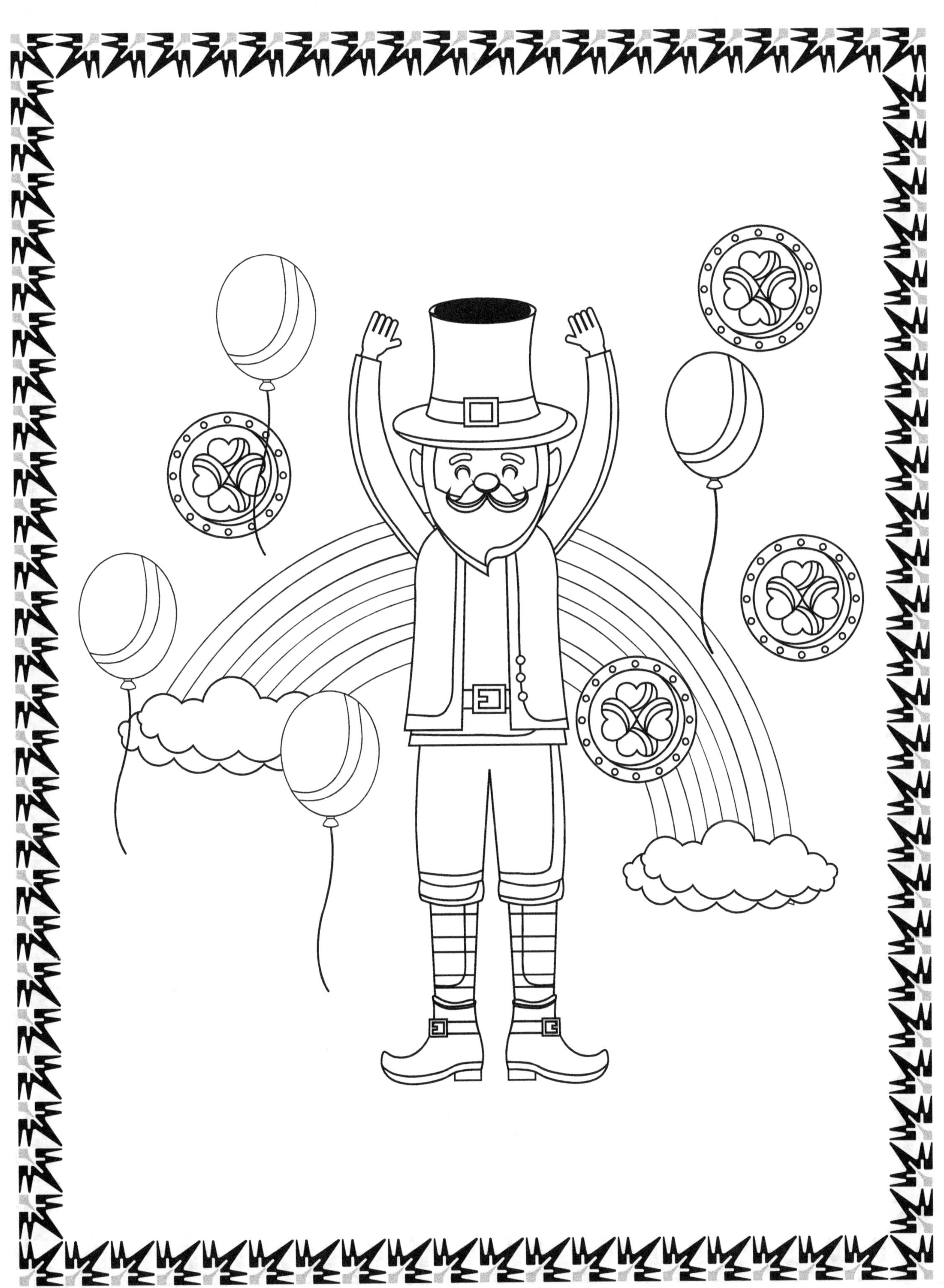

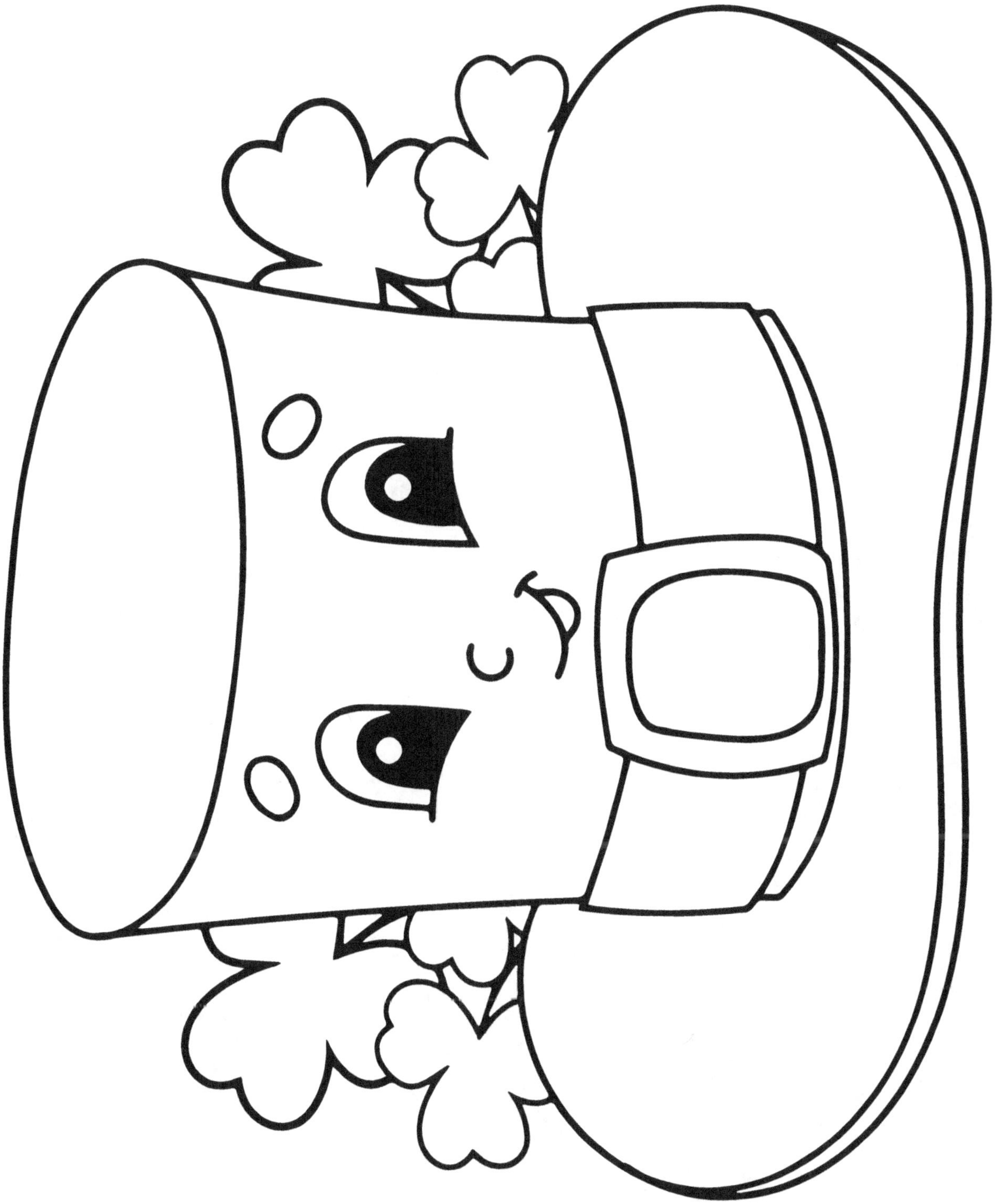

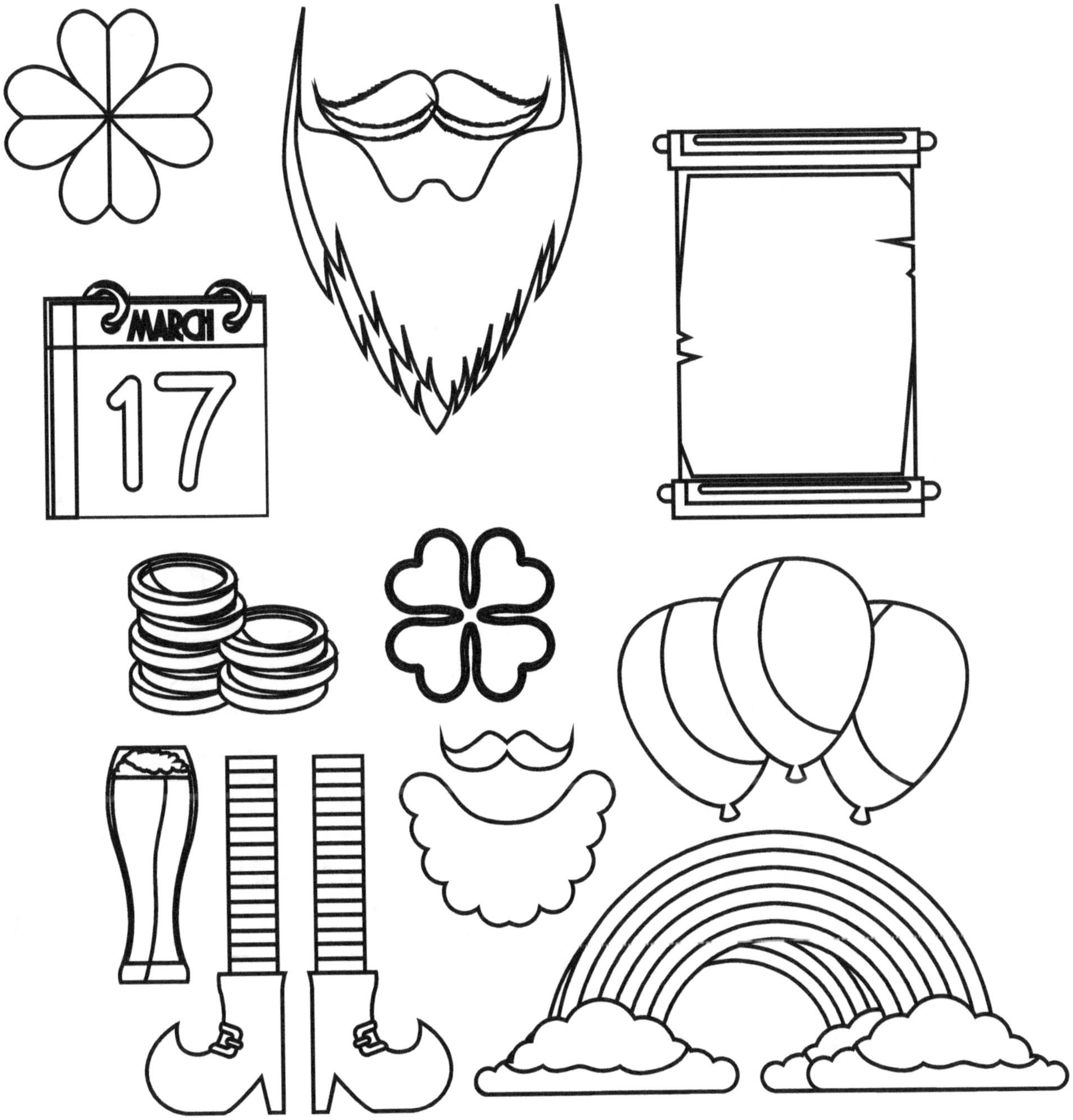

MARCH
17

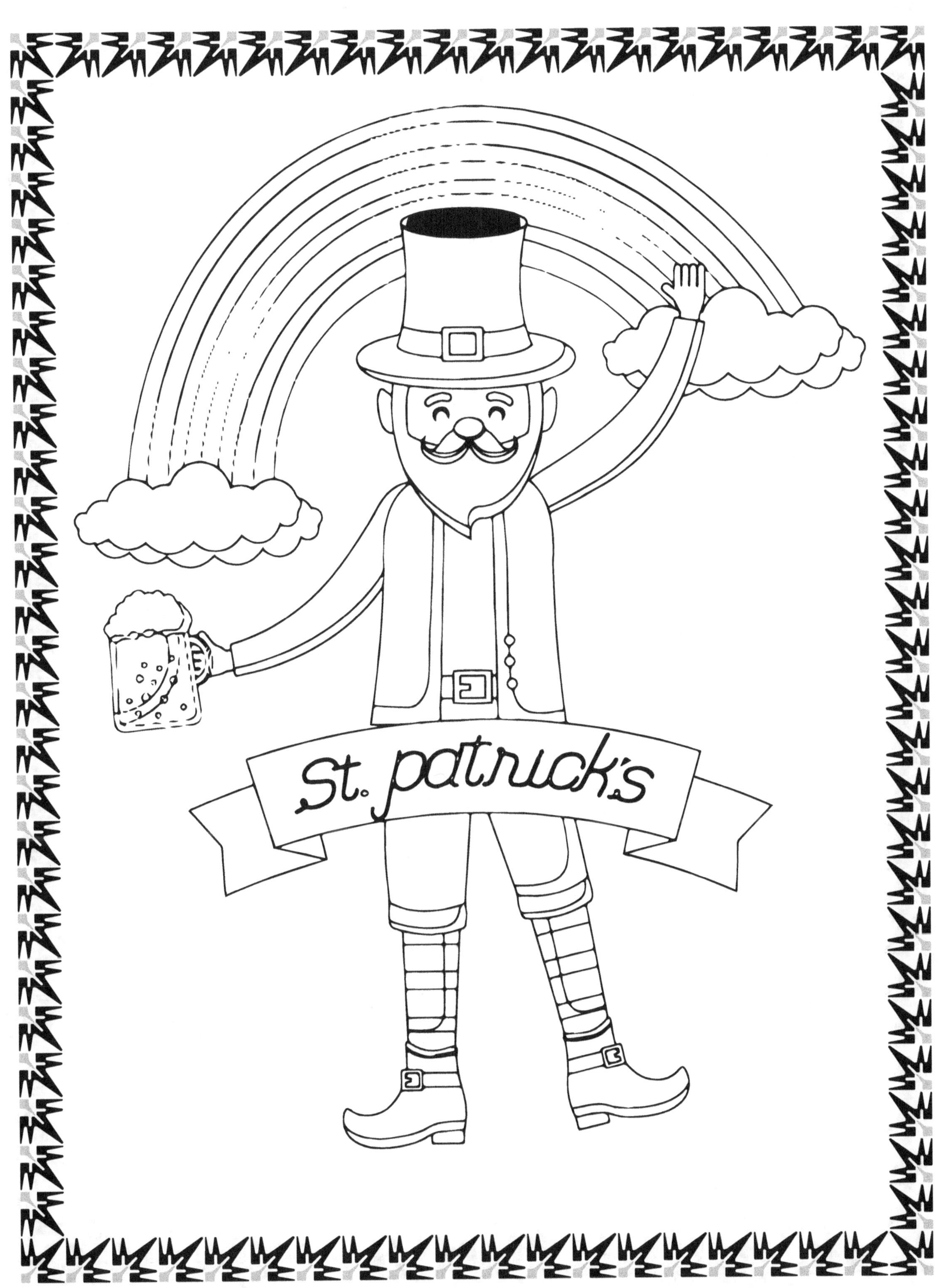

St. patrick's

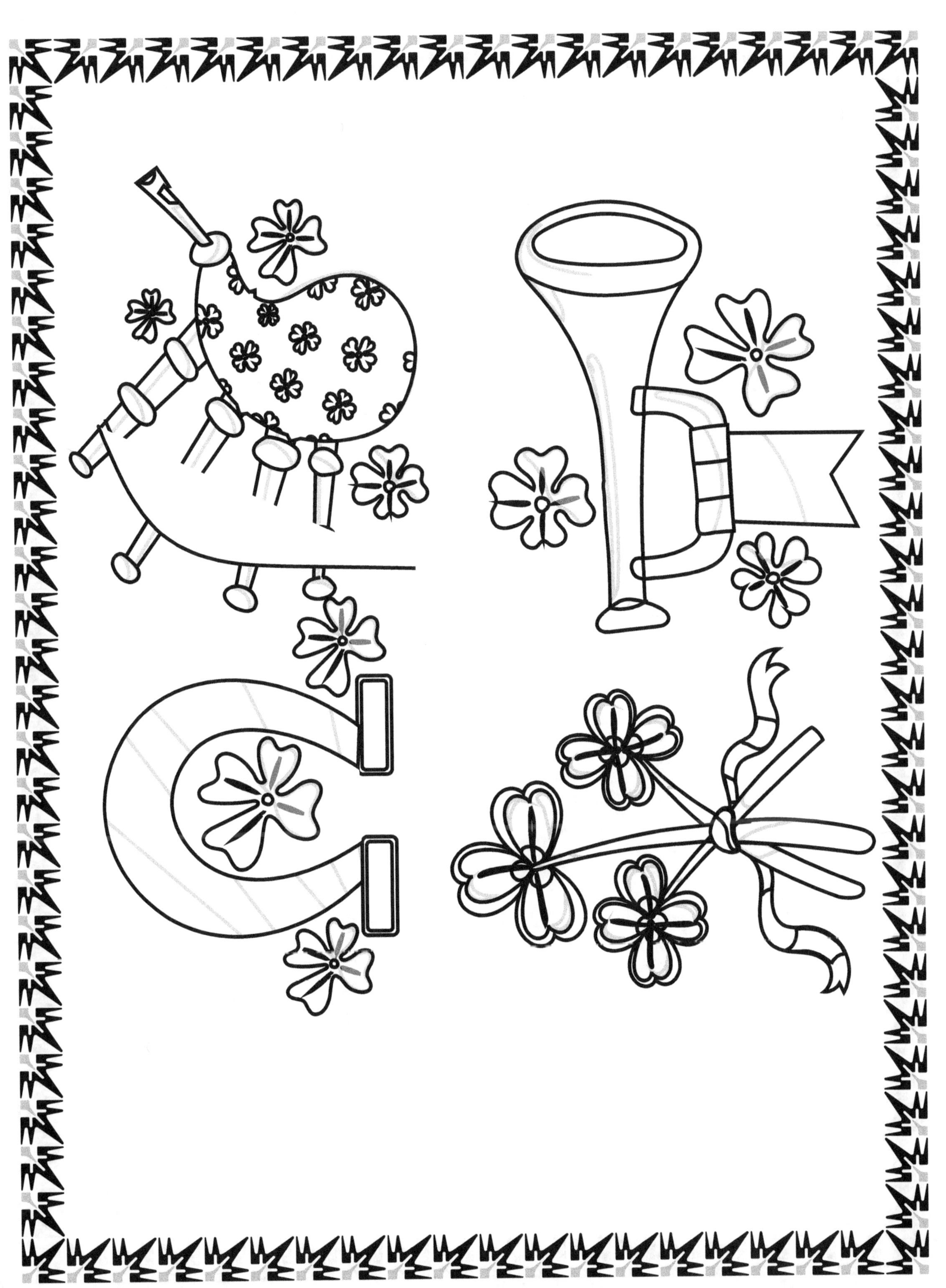

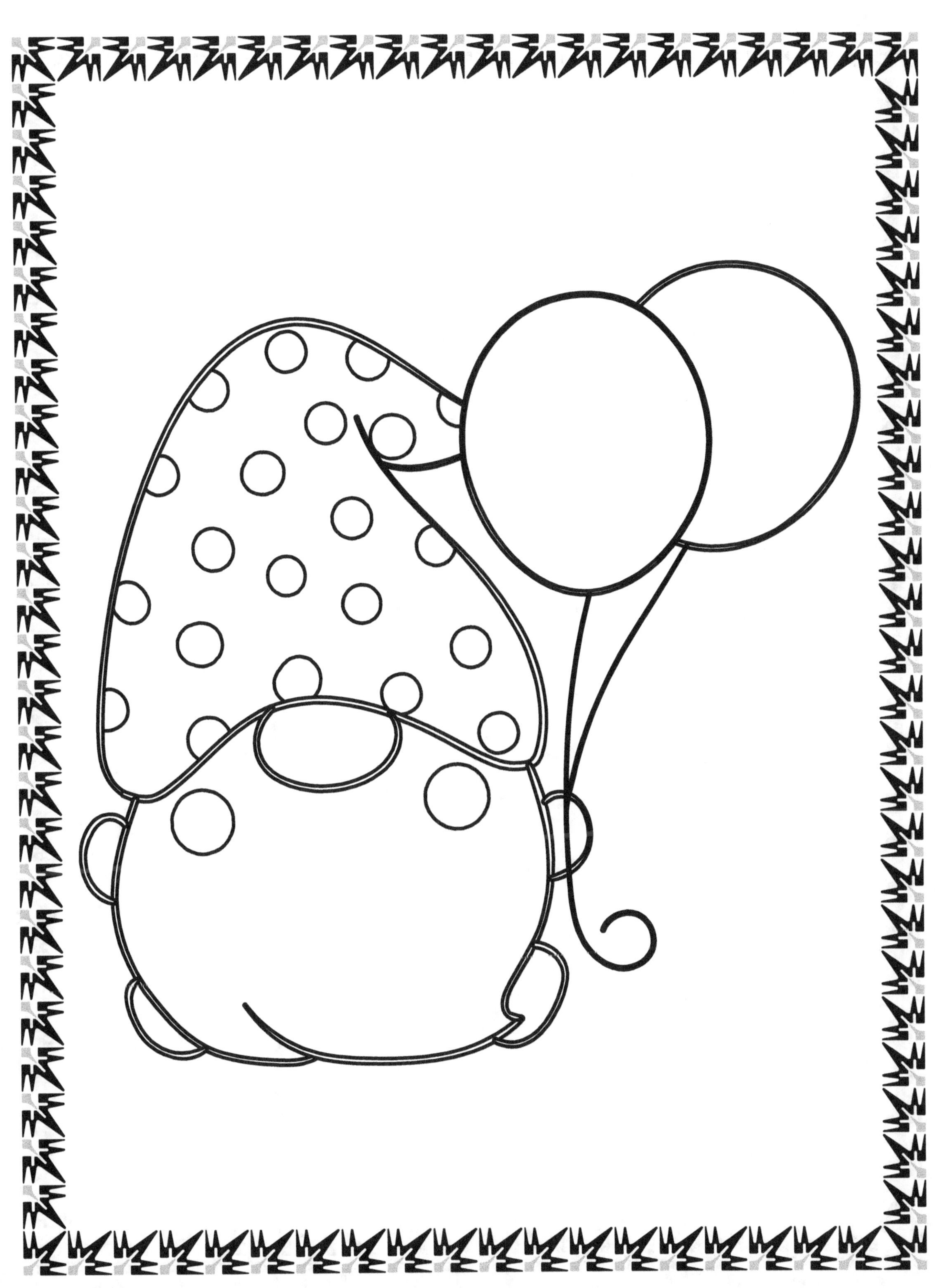

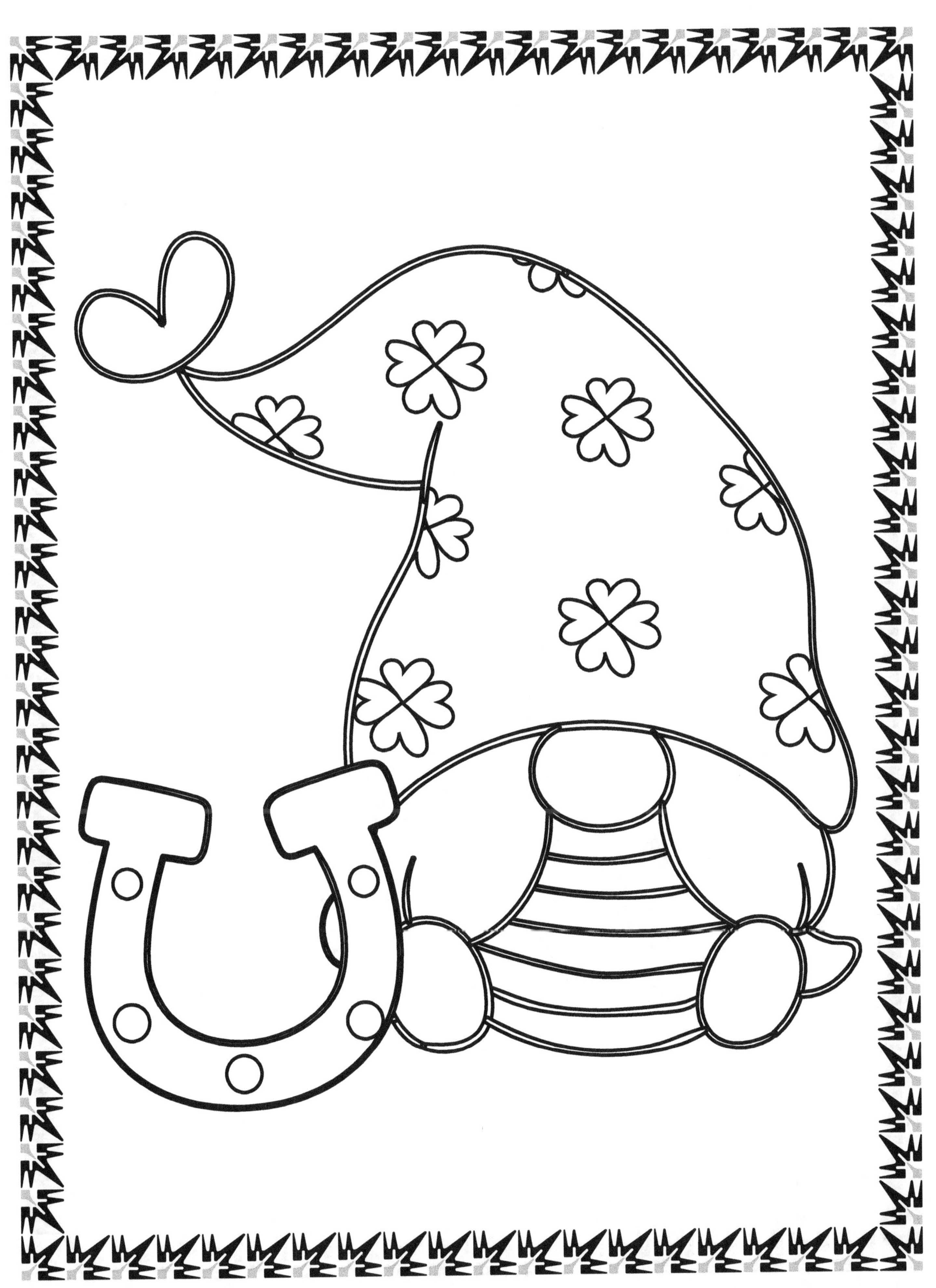

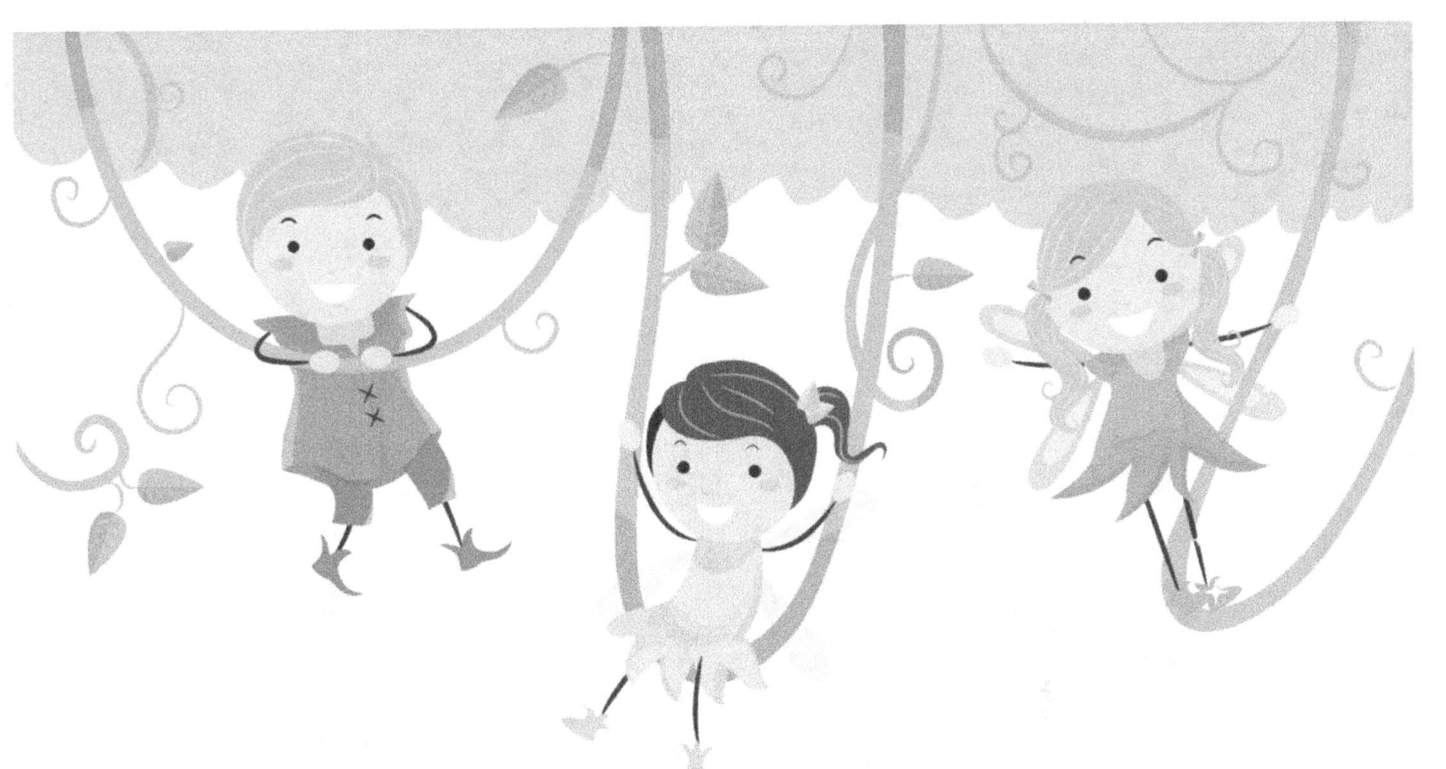

HEY, WE WANT TO HEAR FROM YOU!

PLEASE LEAVE A REVIEW BECAUSE WE WOULD LOVE TO KNOW YOUR THOUGHT'S

thanks for your support

thank
you